Quit Lying to My Children!

Lida Lee Roberts

Copyright © 2025 *Lida Lee Roberts*

All rights reserved. No portion of this book may be reproduced, stored in a retrieval system, or transmitted in any form or by any means – electronic, mechanical, photocopy, recording, scanning, or other – except for brief quotations in critical reviews or articles, without the prior written permission of the author and copyright holder.

Scripture quotations are taken from the King James Version Bible. Public Domain.

Figure 1 license to reproduce granted by citing the article: Ref: Francesca E. Duncan et al (2016), Scientific Reports http://dx.doi.org/10.1038/srep24737

Table of Contents

Chapter 1 The Hole in Your Heart 1
Chapter 2 The Garden 4
Chapter 3 The Way 8
Chapter 4 Euphoria 14
Chapter 5 The Big Bang! 18
Chapter 6 The Choice 24
Chapter 7 Gentleness 30
Chapter 8 Jesus 41
Chapter 9 The Enemy 54
Chapter 10 The Eye 60
Chapter 11 The Flood 65
Chapter 12 The Not so Great, Not so much a Mystery, Babylon 69
Chapter 13 Godincidences 75
Chapter 14 The Church 79
Chapter 15 The Anti-Christ 86
Chapter 16 The Dragon 92
Chapter 17 The Coat of Many Colors 106
Chapter 18 The Woman at the Well 111
Chapter 19 Kosmos 120

I dedicate this book

First of all, to Jesus Christ, our Lord and Savior, that I pray honors Him and is exactly what He wanted me to write. No more, No less. And I pray I didn't mess it up like we talked about!

To my family and friends whom I love dearly. I changed your names to protect the innocent. Just kidding!

To Antonio and Cinzia at Masseria Usamborgia. To whom the Lord led me. They took me in and fed me and took care of me so that I could be still and write this book. May He bless you richly…

Luke 10:5-9 And into whatsoever house ye enter, first say, Peace be to this house. And if the son of peace be there, your peace shall rest upon it: if not, it shall turn to you again. And in the same house remain, eating and drinking such things as they give: for the labourer is worthy of his hire. Go not from house to house. And into whatsoever city ye enter, and they receive you, eat such things as are set before you: And heal the sick that are therein, and say unto them, The kingdom of God is come nigh unto you.

Proverbs 1:7 The fear of the Lord is the beginning of knowledge: but fools despise wisdom and instruction.

(Fear here can also be translated Reverence)

2 Timothy 3:15-16 And that from a child thou hast known the holy scriptures, which are able to make thee wise unto salvation through faith which is in Christ Jesus. All scripture is given by inspiration of God, and is profitable for doctrine, for reproof, for correction, for instruction in righteousness:

1 Kings 8:41-43 Moreover concerning a stranger, that is not of thy people Israel, but cometh out of a far country for thy name's sake;(For they shall hear of thy great name, and of thy strong hand, and of thy stretched out arm when he shall come and pray toward this house;

Hear thou in heaven thy dwelling place, and do according to all that the stranger calleth to thee for: that all people of the earth may know thy name, to fear thee, as do thy people Israel; and that they may know that this house, which I have builded, is called by thy name.

Foreword

God allowed me to take the picture on the cover of this book in March of 2023. Most of that story is in Chapter 8 – Jesus for those of you who like to skip ahead. The Holy Spirit stirred me to write this book, knowing that the picture wouldn't be believable without the story in this age of artificial intelligence.

He has also given me visions and knowledge of things to share with you, along with my own personal testimonies to hopefully squelch the crazy factor. I say that because I know some of it sounds unbelievable, I still think that myself reading and reflecting on everything. But, it is all true and divinely inspired for all of us.

The bible describes Jesus coming in the clouds, which you can see in the picture. When that happens for real. When He comes to reclaim the earth and set everything back in perfect order as it was. Including you and me…. We have to be ready.

We have to make ourselves ready for the bridegroom as a chaste virgin having not worshipped anything else besides God. No other false idols. We need to have faith in Christ and know the Word of God. Which are one in the same. I will go into all of this more in the coming chapters, but I believe God allowed me to take that picture to tell you that you need to GET READY NOW. Repent of your sins, turn to Jesus and love Him and study your bibles. It's not a lot to ask. There is a day coming when it is a day too late, and He will shut the door on you and say I never knew you.

It has taken me a long time to realize the depth of God's love for me (and you). I don't think we can truly grasp it until we get to heaven. But this life is a beautiful scavenger hunt where He leaves little crumbs of miracles to slowly uncover Himself, His love and even more amazing who YOU are.

YOU ARE A CHILD OF GOD

Whether you believe it or not is irrelevant and doesn't change that fact. Whether you acknowledge Him in your life or not, He still loves you. He has been chasing you for centuries and you are his lost sheep. He will leave the ninety-nine to go after the ONE.

You are the reason we are still here and not in the garden. He wants all of his children with Him. And we will continue to live this life with satan and his fallen angels until all have been converted and found.

Satan is the only one that is condemned. The only one... it was his pride that caused him to fall. But he won't repent and considers himself as God. Everything else is forgivable with repentance...

I know that is a hard thing to understand. Our instinct is to judge others and ourselves. But think about it. God created all of those individuals and only He knows their heart... their upbringing... their mental issues... He is the potter. We aren't to question and definitely it is not for us to judge. He weaves everything! Even the bad stuff for the good of those who love Him.

Have Faith.

There is a LOT of scripture quoted in here because that is how God reveals Himself to me, and to anyone really. The Holy Spirit will start to put in your mind things that He wants you to study further and pay attention to, if you ask Him, and it is a beautiful hunt for the truth. But you have to have faith, and you have to study for that to happen. Actually, the more you study the more faith you will have as you come more and more into the truth.

John 14:26 But the Comforter, which is the Holy Ghost, whom the Father will send in my name, he shall teach you all things, and bring all things to your remembrance, whatsoever I have said unto you.

I love that He will bring things to your remembrance. You knew these things before. The Word says He has written His laws on your heart and put His words in your mind. I always think of how they say that we really only use about ten percent of our brains. I truly think the other ninety percent will be awakened when we go to Heaven. It will be complete and total recall of all of the beauty that you came from! How cool is that?

Along those same lines when we see color, science tells us that what we are seeing is all of the colors at once except that color. We are really seeing the absence of that color. I believe that to be our blindness in this world caused by sin, separating us from God. There are many references in the bible of the Shakina glory, which is the throne of the Lord. It is all of the colors and brilliance of them at once. Like only the ten percent use of our brains, I think we can only see about that much color. How amazing it will be to see ALL of the colors at once and the beauty of God's Glory and his throne when we get to Heaven!

All of the scripture here is quoted from the King James Bible. If you are inspired after reading this and want to study more in depth. I recommend getting a companion bible that has a running outline to the side that helps keep subject and object straight and offers some help with translations. I'm a big fan of, if it doesn't sound right google what it was, in what language and how it should read. Although that seems to not be as reliable these days, so good to have a concordance (Strongs is a good one) to help you take things back into the original language.

I also quoted the scripture without each individual verse being identified. I did this because even that demarcation is a translation, and I wanted you to read the scriptures together as a whole to absorb the context.

I'm sure that there will be many that disagree with everything I've said or even quoted. I can only share with you what the Holy Spirit shared with me. I ask you to pray for discernment before reading this book and for God to open the eyes of your heart. And, I encourage you to open your bibles and read it for yourselves, and develop that relationship with your Father. He will lead you. He will never forsake you. I love you all, sweet brothers and sisters!

Chapter 1

The Hole in Your Heart

That huge hole in your heart that has always been there is no accident. You were designed that way to be inhabited by the Holy Spirit. He is quite literally the only thing that can ever truly fill you up. Our souls (hearts) are receiving bodies for Him. Much like men and women were designed to fit together physically, so are we with the Holy Spirit spiritually. God goes into that much deeper in the Bible with a wedding that occurs at the end times when Christ returns, but we will get into that much later…

That hole is there no matter what you do. You can fill it momentarily with fleeting happiness from relationships, kids, jobs, house etc. But those things will also always frustrate you eventually. Because they are not perfect and news flash, neither are you!

You can never find lasting, fulfilling joy, forever and ever through another person or anything else in this world. And no matter how young or old or how rich or poor, you know this to be true in your heart and soul. Because you have experienced heartbreak and disappointment from everything in your life at some point. Usually from the same things that brought you happiness at one time. This life is constant change and that is very unsettling. Our souls were not made for that…

If we continually search for that joy in other things besides God (what we were made and designed for), that is what causes addiction in my opinion. It is a form of insanity that we all do… running from thing to thing to try and make ourselves feel complete.

Most people think of addiction as drug problems, alcohol, food, sex… the "bad" stuff. But I think it is literally anything that we seek to put in that hole… anything that we put above God which can include your kids, spouse, family, house, job, money, whatever! And friends, anything you put above God is an idol and God views it as sin.

I know that sounds harsh, but it is true…

Matthew 10:37-39 He that loveth father or mother more than me is not worthy of me: and he that loveth son or daughter more than me is not worthy of me. And he that taketh not his cross, and followeth after me, is not worthy of me.

Jesus also said in:

Matthew 22:37-40 Jesus said unto him, Thou shalt love the Lord thy God with all thy heart, and with all thy soul, and with all thy mind. This is the first and great commandment. And the second is like unto it, Thou shalt love thy neighbour as thyself. On these two commandments hang all the law and the prophets.

Ponder that deeply for a moment… Let go of how this world has taught you to view sin and judge others. How it has taught you to put yourself above everything.

On those two commandments about love hang some of the law? No, ALL of it. Did it say anything about except murder, homosexuality, adulterers, thieves? No, ALL of it. That means if you are not doing those two things you are just as bad as those other guys in God's eyes.

Sin is sin to God.

I don't think he has varying degrees like we do. Judging homosexuals when committing adultery for instance. Our churches have their own brand of judgement which has driven many people away from the church. The church should be the ultimate expression of Commandment number two, love thy neighbor as thyself! But they often create an atmosphere, where if you are not living the "Christian" life, you are shunned. I put to you, that is a worse sin than any of them. That is putting yourself to be God.

Matthew 7:1-5 Judge not, that you be not judged. For with what judgment you judge, you will be judged; and with the measure you use, it will be measured back to you. And why do you look at the speck in your brother's eye, but do not consider the plank in your own eye? Or how can you say to your brother, 'Let me remove the speck from your eye'; and look, a plank is in your own eye? Hypocrite! First remove the plank from your own eye, and then you will see clearly to remove the speck from your brother's eye.

Knowing that we all suffer from the same sickness… that hole in our heart. Hopefully, you can begin to see that we are all just trying to fill it up. To heal ourselves. Each with different idols and none is better or worse than the other. That goes back to number two again… Love your neighbor as yourself because he is just as sick as you are. Brokenhearted. THAT is the type of Godly compassion that He wants us to have for each other. AND, to encourage each other to turn back to our God as number one in our lives.

I love you all and God has asked me to write this to you… in His perfect love.

Chapter 2

The Garden

I woke up in the middle of the night and fell to my knees in my mind, even though I was blind and could only see black. In my brain or soul, not really sure which, I knew exactly where I was. Even stranger is, I had been there before.

I began to cry and exclaim "I am so sorry… I am so sorry… I know it is so beautiful, but I am not ready yet. I am so sorry…" With that, a voice sort of surrounded me and came from inside me (not speaking to or at me) and said, "Read about me and you won't be afraid".

With that I woke up stunned. I then realized that I had an incredible pain in my chest. I knew that I had suffered a heart attack, but I wasn't afraid. I knew I would be fine and had just been briefly taken to be in His presence. Which He I don't know… Father, Son, Holy Spirit. But I belonged, and was a part of His energy, as He was and is mine now that I am aware of it.

Then came a flood of doubts. What the heck was that? Was I dreaming? What does He want me to do with that? How do I not disappoint Him? Why would He visit me? I really just sort of freaked out for a while. But deep down, I knew it was real.

I wasn't a part of a church at the time and ended up reaching out to a pastor online that I followed on social media. I explained to him what had happened. He helped me to understand that I might not truly fathom the meaning of that in weeks, months, years or even this lifetime.

I would later understand that it would be integral in the testimony of my whole life. He did state that it reminded him of the story of Peter walking on water. He was fine as long as he kept his gaze on Jesus, but as soon as he looked away, he started to sink. As soon as we put our focus on this world, the waters of this life can sweep us away.

The voice of God will never be the voice of fear in your life. Cast the devil away from you in Jesus' name, which He gave you power to do as a believer and put your focus back on Christ. This can be a daily exercise in times of testing. This is true for all of us with Him, but this has really held true for me ever since that experience in my life.

A couple of weeks later, I stumbled across a website that touted a daily reading plan to read the entire bible in a year. I sent an email to everyone I knew… I didn't share my experience because I thought people would think I was crazy. But I committed to doing it and promised to send a daily email with the scriptures to everyone who wanted to do it with me.

I did great for a while but must admit that I fell behind and didn't complete the reading. I did finish sending the emails every day. I know this planted a lot of seeds with my friends and family and for that I am very proud and feel that was part of what God wanted me to do after the visitation.

After my father passed away, I became much more focused on studying the bible. I have committed my life to it and Jesus now (again). I know it is a guide to us directly inspired from God. It is intended to show us how to live on this earth with peace in the Holy Spirit. I also now have a ministry of my own teaching the word of God, which brings me great joy and has brought purpose to my life.

The bible was written by forty different authors over fifteen hundred years!! Think about that!

How can such continuity be accomplished by that many people over that long of a period if not divinely inspired? I think the biggest testament that shows it is true is to look at the Psalms written by King David. Psalms 22 describes some of the events that take place at the crucifixion. This was written a thousand years before Christ was crucified. How in the world can that happen except through God.

Examples:

Psalm 22:1 My God, my God, why hast thou forsaken me?

Matthew 27:46 And about the ninth hour Jesus cried with a loud voice, saying, Eli, Eli, lama sabachthani? that is to say, My God, my God, why hast thou forsaken me?

Psalm 22:7-8 All they that see me laugh me to scorn: they shoot out the lip, they shake the head, saying, He trusted on the LORD that he would deliver him: let him deliver him, seeing he delighted in him.

Matthew 27:39-43 And they that passed by reviled him, wagging their heads, And saying, Thou that destroyest the temple, and buildest it in three days, save thyself. If thou be the Son of God, come down from the cross. Likewise also the chief priests mocking him, with the scribes and elders, said, He saved others; himself he cannot save. If he be the King of Israel, let him now come down from the cross, and we will believe him. He trusted in God; let him deliver him now, if he will have him: for he said, I am the Son of God.

Psalm 22:14-18 I am poured out like water, and all my bones are out of joint: my heart is like wax; it is melted in the midst of my bowels. My strength is dried up like a potsherd; and my tongue cleaveth to my jaws; and thou hast brought me into the dust of death. For dogs have compassed me: the assembly of the wicked have inclosed me: they pierced my hands and my feet. I may tell all my bones: they look and stare upon me. They part my garments among them, and cast lots upon my vesture.

Matthew 27:35-36 And they crucified him, and parted his garments, casting lots: that it might be fulfilled which was spoken by the prophet, They parted my garments among them, and upon my vesture did they cast lots. And sitting down they watched him there;

Another prophecy seven hundred years before Jesus was Isaiah:

Isaiah 53:3-10 He is despised and rejected of men; a man of sorrows, and acquainted with grief: and we hid as it were our faces from him; he was despised, and we esteemed him not. Surely he hath borne our griefs, and carried our sorrows: yet we did esteem him stricken, smitten of God, and afflicted. But he was wounded for our transgressions, he was bruised for our iniquities: the chastisement of our peace was upon him; and with his stripes we are healed. All we like sheep have gone astray; we have turned every one to his own way; and the Lord hath laid on him the iniquity of us all. He was oppressed, and he was afflicted, yet he opened not his mouth: he is brought as a lamb to the slaughter, and as a sheep before her shearers is dumb, so he openeth not his mouth. He was taken from prison and from judgment: and who shall declare his generation? for he was cut off out of the land of the living: for the transgression of my people was he stricken. And he made his grave with the wicked, and with the rich in his death; because he had done no violence, neither was any deceit in his mouth. Yet it pleased the Lord to bruise him; he hath put him to grief: when thou shalt make his soul an offering for sin, he shall see his seed, he shall prolong his days, and the pleasure of the Lord shall prosper in his hand.

Isaiah 7:14 Therefore the Lord himself shall give you a sign; Behold, a virgin shall conceive, and bear a son, and shall call his name Immanuel.

Immanuel means God with us. I think that speaks for itself… Praise the Lord.

Chapter 3

The Way

John 14:6 Jesus saith unto him, I am the way, the truth, and the life: no man cometh unto the Father, but by me.

He meant that… He meant every word that He ever said, and it will all come to its fulfilment. ALL of it. I used to think that as long as you believe in God, it didn't matter what religion or how you worshipped. That was just how you were taught. But, that's not what it says.

NO ONE COMES TO THE FATHER BUT BY ME. Period.

John 1:1-4 In the beginning was the Word, and the Word was with God, and the Word was God. The same was in the beginning with God. All things were made by him; and without him was not any thing made that was made. In him was life; and the life was the light of men. And the light shineth in darkness; and the darkness comprehended it not.

That first verse is hard for us to comprehend I think in our limited flesh brains. The Word was God and has been around since the beginning.

John 1:14 And the Word was made flesh, and dwelt among us, (and we beheld his glory, the glory as of the only begotten of the Father,) full of grace and truth.

God literally sent His word, His Son, Himself to you to rescue you and teach you how to survive in these flesh bodies and to KNOW Him. That is the entire purpose of your existence in this life. To come to know Jesus and be perfected in Him so you can live in eternity forever with Him. Without that, you cannot be in His holy presence and will die.

And how do you know Him? Through the Word. When Jesus taught us to take communion at the last supper. He said this is my body broken for you. Eat it. He was talking about the Word of God. "The Word was made flesh and dwelt among us". You are expected to "eat" it. When He said this is my blood. Drink it. He was talking about your inheritance into that blood family. How beautiful it is.

Matthew 26:26-28 And as they were eating, Jesus took bread, and blessed it, and brake it, and gave it to the disciples, and said, Take, eat; this is my body. And he took the cup, and gave thanks, and gave it to them, saying, Drink ye all of it; For this is my blood of the new testament, which is shed for many for the remission of sins.

You may think you have other priorities in this life. I hear people quote the following verse a lot in the sense that God just wants us to be happy.

Psalm 37:4 Delight yourself in the Lord and He will give you the desires of your heart.

God does want to give you the desires of your heart. But our flesh confuses what that is. It is not a Christmas list that we pray, and he gives us everything on it like Santa. The desire of your heart, whether you know it or not is Him. Again, only He can fill that hole where He was designed to be.

I remember as a child my mom asking her best friend who was dying in the hospital if she had ever felt truly loved. That confused me because she was married and had kids! What on earth was she talking about?

But I understand now… There is only one thing in this life that will give you that security and eternal and complete love. That is your relationship with your heavenly Father. He is your creator and your closest relative, father and husband. No one will ever love you and understand you like he does. He is the creator and lover of your soul. Not this body but your everlasting soul… the essence of you that you don't even know or understand in these flesh bodies.

The bible is God's love letter to you. Do you remember that book going around several years ago talking about knowing you and your partner's love languages? This is His love language to you! And yours back to Him, when you read it and pray for understanding. It will fulfill your every need and give you true and lasting Joy.

The desires of your heart are to be in love with Jesus…To be in a holy marriage with Him, forever! If you don't understand that holy marriage yet, just put it on the shelf for now…

If I had a pill and gave it to you and told you that it would solve ALL of your problems. Would you take it? Of course you would! THIS IS THAT PILL!

Ecclesiastes 1:14 I have seen all the works that are done under the sun; and, behold, all is vanity and vexation of spirit.

That is why you are sick and unsteady in this world always… but,

2 Corinthians 5:17 Therefore if any man be in Christ, he is a new creature: old things are passed away; behold, all things are become new.

The bible is literally an owner's manual on how to live in these flesh bodies. Would you operate your car without reading the manual? Well, many of us do… Maybe that's a bad analogy. Would you try to put something together from IKEA without using the directions? You shouldn't live without reading how to live right!

Practically every page is an assurance and promise of love on the beautiful forever you will have with the love of your life! IF (a lot of preachers skip over that part) you repent of your sins and ask forgiveness for them and love the Lord your God with all of your heart and soul and mind AND, love your neighbor as yourself. You have to turn completely to God… the Jews call it teshuvah. It's not only asking for forgiveness, repentance, but to return completely as if going back to something that you have strayed or looks away from. You are not able to do this of your own power. You need to pray for that desire and strength as well.

Philippians 2:13 God is working in you, giving you the desire to obey Him and the power to do what pleases Him.

Studying the bible is not only obedience, but it brings God JOY!

Nehemiah 8:10 For the Joy of the Lord is your strength

And when you are strong in the Lord, it brings you joy! Not fleeting happiness as earthly pleasures, but life giving, sustainable soul joy. That's what He wants for you and the only way to experience that is to know the Father and the only way to know Him is to study His Word.

That joy is also contagious! That joy that you spread brings fruit. Joy is the oil that never runs out… It flows to us and through us to others and back to our Father and back down to us in a beautiful joyful perfect circle of LIFE!!

Before the first trip that I will be discussing in the next chapters, I watched a movie called "The Way". It's funny how Jesus guides us to things. This is a movie from 2011 with Emilio Estevez and Martin Sheen. I had three people bring it up in conversation within the same week and then it was suggested to me on Netflix. Duh. I guess I need to watch it.

It was about a man who lost his son, and he had to go recover his body. The son had been doing the walk of the Camino de Santiago, which is a pilgrimage route through France, Portugal and Spain that ends at the supposed burial place of the apostle James. He ends up completing the walk with the ashes of his son. But, "the way" is about all of the lives that he touched and that touched his along "the way". How every connection, no matter how brief, matters; and is divinely woven into this tapestry of our lives.

Have you ever considered that we are all still stuck here in this God forsaken place because God is waiting on you? Or your father, mother, husband, kid, neighbor, cashier, mechanic, friend, co-worker? Anyone that you have been assigned to plant a seed with. If you think one seed from you can not only help God get that one, but help bring in God's Kingdom faster wouldn't you be rushing to do it? We are not only responsible for ourselves, but each other. The Lord even told Ezekiel if you knew what was coming and didn't warn the people, their blood was on your hands.

Ezekiel 33:6 But if the watchman see the sword come, and blow not the trumpet, and the people be not warned; if the sword come, and take any person from among them, he is taken away in his iniquity; but his blood will I require at the watchman's hand.

Jesus instructed us to teach the Word of God. That is what they call the great commission:

Matthew 28:18-20 And Jesus came and spake unto them, saying, All power is given unto me in heaven and in earth. Go ye therefore, and teach all nations, baptizing them in the name of the Father, and of the Son, and of the Holy Ghost: Teaching them to observe all things whatsoever I have commanded you: and, lo, I am with you always, even unto the end of the world. Amen.

The fact that we aren't all in spiritual bodies with Jesus means there are still strays out there!

I've always studied but I haven't always seeked Him. Those are two very different things. I grew up going to Sunday School and went to Baptist high school and college. I studied intellectually but not really to know Him.

Luke 11:9 And I say unto you, Ask, and it shall be given you; seek, and ye shall find; knock, and it shall be opened unto you.

If you ask Him, the Holy Spirit will reveal to you what He wants you to know every day. He will give you just enough... I think if He were to give us everything at the same time our heads would pop off. Give us this day our daily bread isn't just for physical food, but spiritual food. And you do need to feast on it every day to stay connected to Him.

John 6:57-58 As the living Father hath sent me, and I live by the Father: so he that eateth me, even he shall live by me. This is that bread which came down from heaven: not as your fathers did eat manna, and are dead: he that eateth of this bread shall live for ever.

The word for disciple in both Hebrew and Greek means a student. That is what you are called to be all of the days of your life. A student of God's word. Like Mary sitting at the feet of Jesus while Martha was working. She chose wisely. And so should you.

Did you know that there are over seven thousand promises in the word of God?

Psalms 145:13 The Lord is faithful to all His promises and loving toward all He has made.

Deuteronomy 31:8 The Lord HIMSELF goes before you and will be with you. He will never leave you or forsake you.

He even says:

Isaiah 43:26 Put me in remembrance: let us plead together: declare thou, that thou mayest be justified.

Do you think He forgot His promises? Of course not! He wants to know that you have studied and understand how much He loves you so He can call you His own and justify you. Then he can give you the desires of your heart which is literally and figuratively HIM!

How precious it is.

Chapter 4

Euphoria

I was about 5 years old… we had a wonderful place at the coast in Port Aransas, Texas. We would go down there several times a year. This time was in the winter and as is common in Texas we had a very warm day despite being very cold the days previous.

I wanted to go swimming and would not give up on it despite my parents saying it was too cold. My dad finally said I'll just take her down there and let her put her toes in. Of course, I never do anything like that… I was so excited that I ran and jumped into the deep end of the pool.

As soon as I hit the water, it was so cold that my body immediately went into shock. I remember everything was in extremely slow motion. I began to sink as I couldn't move or breathe.

You would think that your fight or flight would kick in and you would be panicking. That is not what happened.

I felt the most peaceful euphoria of my young and inexperienced life. It was pure happiness and love. No fear whatsoever. Extremely calming and sweet. It seemed like a long time that I was wrapped up in that love.

My dad was able to grab me and pull me out by my hair. (That was all that he could grab a hold of) I was shivering and in shock. He wrapped me in a towel and took me to my mom upstairs who immediately gave me a shot of whiskey to warm me up. Yes, whiskey. Welcome to my family! But it worked, and I was fine. I would never forget that feeling though…

I had a LOT of fun in college and am very blessed to have made some life-long friends there. It was a wonderful time of my life, but it was not without tragedy.

My roommate and I were dating roommates down the street at the time. She and her boyfriend had talked about getting married and were very much in love.

One evening, they were coming back from a visit with his mom in Dallas. The driver of an 18-wheeler on I-35 fell asleep and the truck jumped the median and literally ran over their car. He was killed instantly. She barely had room for her head in the crushed car and it was a miracle that she survived. She would have to undergo several surgeries and go through a very long recovery. I don't think she has still recovered fully emotionally or physically for that matter.

This was before cell phones. Being in college, I was NEVER home and always out doing something. I believe this was even a Friday or Saturday, which makes it even crazier that I was home to receive the call.

I had forgotten something at home and had only swung by the apartment to get it. I don't remember now what it was, but I was there to take the call from her parents. They were coming from Houston which would take several hours, and they asked me to get to the hospital, which I did. I know that was God that coordinated me to be home for that phone call.

Several months later after she was out of the hospital, my boyfriend and I were coming back from a wedding in Dallas as well. Ironically, we had stopped to call her because we were running late and didn't want her to worry as she was still traumatized and we were on the same stretch of road. We talked to her and told her we were fine and should be there in about an hour.

My boyfriend was driving my car. We had stopped in a very small town, and it was getting dark. Getting back onto the highway, we were both looking behind us for any cars coming as we were merging. All of a sudden there was an impact, and we couldn't see anything but fiery liquid on the windshield.

We pulled over and my boyfriend screamed to get out and run. Which he did… I went to do the same but apparently the impact was on my side of the car so I couldn't open my door. I was in shock so I couldn't figure out how to get out of my seatbelt and get out of the car. I just sat there watching the flames…

Again… that same feeling as when I was drowning in the pool as a child came over me again. I wasn't afraid, it was so peaceful and loving. A feeling honestly that you didn't really want to leave. Better than anything in this life and truly somehow your nature. I don't know if that makes sense, but it is where you belong. Wrapped in love with no fear.

Again, time stopped there, and it seemed like I was there a very long time. In reality, it was probably only a couple of minutes before my boyfriend realized I wasn't behind him. He came back and got me out of my seatbelt and pulled me through the driver's side door. We both fell into the highway, which is amazing we didn't get hit as this is I-35. It is one of the most crowded highways in the US.

We then began running up the median as we were afraid that the car was going to blow up as it was still on fire. Someone finally called 911 and stopped. That's when we realized that we had hit a man walking with a gas can in the entrance to the highway.

There isn't a word for how we felt. He was killed instantly and they later realized that he was drunk. That was likely why he was in the middle of the entrance ramp on the highway. But that didn't matter… it was still a life and something I will never forget.

We were pretty much there all night while they investigated. They later cleaned off my windshield and put the bumper in the back of my Blazer. I had to drive that car back home with my catatonic boyfriend in the passenger seat. A very long silent drive…

We get back to my apartment and almost immediately my mom calls and says "what's wrong?" She said that she had been up making coffee since about midnight. Which is almost exactly when the wreck happened, and she just knew something was wrong. My parents drove up to take care of us, which we desperately needed. They also told my boyfriend how happy they were that he was driving my car and taking care of me.

I don't think death is anything to be afraid of… It is going back home.

Ecclesiastes 12:7 Then shall the dust return to the earth as it was: and the spirit shall return unto God who gave it.

Chapter 5

The Big Bang!

Isaiah 40:21-23 Have ye not known? have ye not heard? hath it not been told you from the beginning? have ye not understood from the foundations of the earth? It is he that sitteth upon the circle of the earth, and the inhabitants thereof are as grasshoppers; that stretcheth out the heavens as a curtain, and spreadeth them out as a tent to dwell in: That bringeth the princes to nothing; he maketh the judges of the earth as vanity.

Have you ever seen a video of when a sperm enters an egg at the exact point of conception? There is a ring of bright light that surrounds it in a beautiful chain reaction that encircles the egg in light and consumes it. The video is much better but here is a picture.

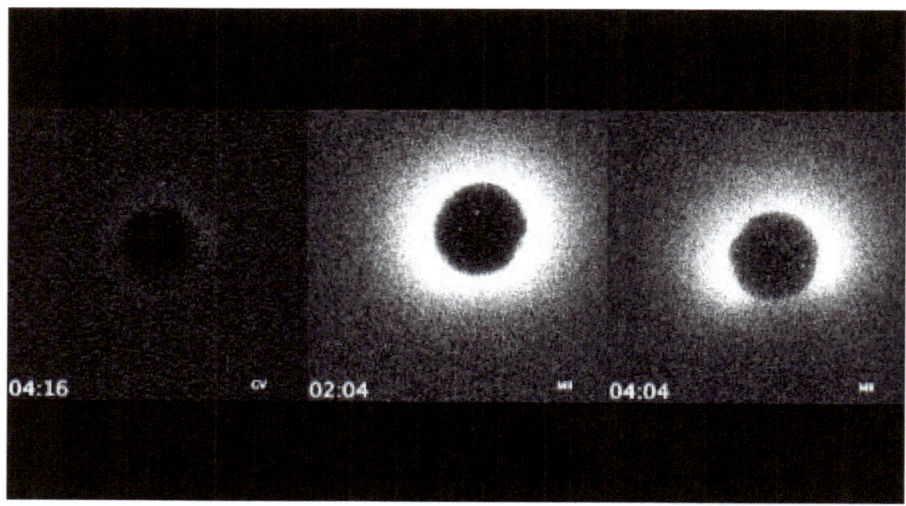

Figure 1 Ref: Francesca E. Duncan et al (2016), Scientific Reports
http://dx.doi.org/10.1038/srep24737

I believe that to be the "big bang" that science talks about in the beginning. Except it was God's moment of conception of this world. Most things in the bible have varying levels of meaning which allows for the Holy Spirit's lifetime teaching of all of those things to us. Especially parallel in much of the scripture, is us and this earth. It makes sense as we came from dust, right?

Did you know that it states in the bible that one day with the Lord is a thousand years to us?

2 Peter 3: 8 But, beloved, be not ignorant of this one thing, that one day is with the Lord as a thousand years, and a thousand years as one day.

It makes the story of creation make a whole lot more sense, doesn't it? God is very natural… He created it… ALL of it. That moment of the conception of a human being is the same spark or bang if you will that was the conception/creation of this world.

Genesis 1:1-5 In the beginning God created the heaven and the earth. And the earth was without form, and void; and darkness was upon the face of the deep. And the Spirit of God moved upon the face of the waters. And God said, Let there be light: and there was light. And God saw the light, that it was good: and God divided the light from the darkness. And God called the light Day, and the darkness he called Night. And the evening and the morning were the first day.

Look at the first two lines above from Genesis. God created the heaven and the earth, and the earth was without form and void. Those words without form and void are translated in Hebrew, tohu va-vohu, which literally means to lay waste, a dry desert without water.

Why did God create something and then lay waste to it? I'll give you one guess… Lucifer/Satan.

Hebrews 11:3 Through faith we understand that the worlds were framed by the word of God, so that things which are seen were not made of things which do appear.

Knowing Jesus IS the word of God all things were framed in Him. In His image.

Ephesians 2:20-21 And are built upon the foundation of the apostles and prophets, Jesus Christ himself being the chief corner stone; In whom all the building fitly framed together groweth unto an holy temple in the Lord:

That word "worlds" in that verse from Hebrews is aion in the Greek, which means eon or ages. In other words, the world ages not worlds. God only created this world once. He only framed it in Jesus once. But has had to destroy it, flood it and will destroy it again before restoring it back to its original perfection with His children. All of this to save His children.

There are two words primarily used in the bible translated as "foundation". Themelios is primarily used in association with Jesus Christ as our foundation. Katabole is primarily used in reference to this world or Kosmos in the Greek and it means a lot more than just "foundation".

katabolē 1) a throwing or laying down. 1a) the injection or depositing of the virile semen in the womb. 1b) of the seed of plants and animals. 2) a founding (laying down a foundation)

kata means down from, through, against, according to, towards, during

bole in Greek means to throw, send or put

Side note: I think it's interesting that in English bole means the trunk of a tree. Think about it… in the beginning in the garden there were two trees.

Have you ever looked at a map of the world? It almost looks like the pieces could be shoved back together perfectly to make one land mass. Like someone just shook the pieces a part. God destroyed this world before this current earth age in a katabole.

Hebrews 12:26 Whose voice then shook the earth: but now he hath promised, saying, Yet once more I shake not the earth only, but also heaven.

He is not talking about the flood here. He is talking about "shaking the earth". The earth was not made void by the flood. I know because after the flood, a dove brought an olive branch back to Noah to let him know it was safe to come off of the boat.

Genesis 8:11 And the dove came in to him in the evening; and, lo, in her mouth was an olive leaf pluckt off: so Noah knew that the waters were abated from off the earth.

People get all riled up about how the bible and science are in conflict with each other. The katabole explains most of it right there. Yes, there were dinosaurs and an ice age. It's talked about in Job.

Job 40:14-18 Behold now behemoth, which I made with thee; he eateth grass as an ox. Lo now, his strength is in his loins, and his force is in the navel of his belly. He moveth his tail like a cedar: the sinews of his stones are wrapped together. His bones are as strong pieces of brass; his bones are like bars of iron.

God created this earth age for our salvation. That is why it started with light… Who is our light?

John 8:12 Then spake Jesus again unto them, saying, I am the light of the world: he that followeth me shall not walk in darkness, but shall have the light of life.

Have you ever seen an eclipse? That same chain reaction of light encircles the moon and has the same effect of focusing the light and making it even brighter than it was before. The light overcoming the darkness as it was in the beginning so shall it be in the end. There is another earth age to come. The final one.

The third earth age. And, as always the case, there is more than one meaning. Think of Jesus dead for three days and on the third day rising. So, it must be with us on this earth. We had to be purified with His blood sacrifice to get rid of our sin before we could be reunited with our Creator. God is bringing heaven here and will live here among us. He is not destroying this earth but restoring it back to what it was before Satan's fall. We will go into that more in Chapter 9 – The Enemy.

Revelation 21:1-2 And I saw a new heaven and a new earth: for the first heaven and the first earth were passed away; and there was no more sea. And I John saw the holy city, new Jerusalem, coming down from God out of heaven, prepared as a bride adorned for her husband.

Revelation 21:23 And the city had no need of the sun, neither of the moon, to shine in it: for the glory of God did lighten it, and the Lamb is the light thereof.

Again, it is representative of the earth but also our flesh bodies as it was in the beginning. So, it shall be in the end with the new heaven and our spiritual perfect bodies with Christ conception in us by that light to create our new and perfect selves.

Revelation 21:4 And God shall wipe away all tears from their eyes; and there shall be no more death, neither sorrow, nor crying, neither shall there be any more pain: for the former things are passed away.

John the Baptist told us that we had to be baptized with water and with fire.

Matthew 3:11 I indeed baptize you with water unto repentance. but he that cometh after me is mightier than I, whose shoes I am not worthy to bear: he shall baptize you with the Holy Ghost, and with fire:

As I explained earlier, things have more than one meaning. I believe that baptism by water and fire is true for individuals and also this earth.

We are baptized with water in obedience, to represent our dying to this flesh and belief that we will be raised again with Christ. We are baptized in fire by the Holy Spirit weighing our hearts and raising us into His Spirit.

Deuteronomy 4:24 For the Lord thy God is a consuming fire, even a jealous God.

Hebrews 12:29 For our God is a consuming fire.

He is a consuming fire for his enemies but for those who love him it is a fire in our heart. A beautiful, warming fire of everlasting love.

I found out in Israel that in Acts when it talks about the Holy Spirit coming upon them, they were most likely reading the word of God. I always had been taught they were praying, but Jews pray standing up. These were sitting which makes sense that the Spirit overcame them with tongues of fire as they were reading the word of God. How precious and powerful the Word of God.

Acts 2:1-6 And when the day of Pentecost was fully come, they were all with one accord in one place. And suddenly there came a sound from heaven as of a rushing mighty wind, and it filled all the house where they were sitting. And there appeared unto them cloven tongues like as of fire, and it sat upon each of them. And they were all filled with the Holy Ghost, and began to speak with other tongues, as the Spirit gave them utterance. And there were dwelling at Jerusalem Jews, devout men, out of every nation under heaven. Now when this was noised abroad, the multitude came together, and were confounded, because that every man heard them speak in his own language.

I included the last verse of that because a lot of churches talk about speaking in tongues. But the definition of that by the bible standards, is that the utterance inspired by the Holy Spirit is understood in all languages at once. Not that the speaker has been given something special that no one else understands.

As we have to be baptized, so does this earth also. It had to be cleansed by water with the flood to get rid of that evil generation and start to turn again towards God. It will also be cleansed by fire to make Holy for Christ's everlasting kingdom. And, that fire is the Word of God. Jesus.

2 Peter 3:3-7 Knowing this first, that there shall come in the last days scoffers, walking after their own lusts, And saying, Where is the promise of his coming? for since the fathers fell asleep, all things continue as they were from the beginning of the creation. For this they willingly are ignorant of, that by the word of God the heavens were of old, and the earth standing out of the water and in the water: Whereby the world that then was, being overflowed with water, perished: But the heavens and the earth, which are now, by the same word are kept in store, reserved unto fire against the day of judgment and perdition of ungodly men.

Is this something to be afraid of? Of course not! Did you know that the phrase do not be afraid is in the bible 365 times? A reminder for every day of the year!

He promises to be with us through both of those baptisms, water and fire.

Isaiah 43: 2 When thou passest through the waters, I will be with thee; and through the rivers, they shall not overflow thee: when thou walkest through the fire, thou shalt not be burned; neither shall the flame kindle upon thee.

Chapter 6

The Choice

There were two trees planted in the Garden of Eden. The Tree of Life and the tree of the knowledge of good and evil. The Tree of Life is our Lord and Savior, Jesus Christ. I'll give you three guesses and take away two of who the other tree is... satan. This controversy has been from the beginning and is the reason we live in an unperfect fallen world.

Eve made that choice to allow herself to be seduced by satan. No, it was not an apple that was eaten that day. The bible does not mention the word apple at all.

Genesis 3:13 And the Lord God said unto the woman, What is this that thou hast done? And the woman said, The serpent beguiled me, and I did eat.

The Greek verb that is used in the bible for beguiled here is exapatao, and means to be wholly seduced. Adam was wholly seduced as well.

We are still making that same bad choice. The seduction now is a little less obvious. But, we choose him every day when we prioritize anything over God. That is ultimately choosing satan. And, he is hard at work beguiling you with the things of this world.

Look at your computer and your phones. Where do you spend most of your time? What is the symbolism on those? Is it an apple with a bite of it? Think about it…

Look at Amazon. Almost every product you can think of is now sold on that platform in one form or another. Talk about controlling all of the buying and selling. What does that symbol look like? It looks like a devil's tail to me.

Another particularly disturbing symbol that satan has adopted is the rainbow. God promised mankind after the flood that He would never destroy the earth again by a flood. Do you know what the symbol of that promise is? The Rainbow.

Genesis 9:13-15 I do set my bow in the cloud, and it shall be for a token of a covenant between me and the earth. And it shall come to pass, when I bring a cloud over the earth, that the bow shall be seen in the cloud: And I will remember my covenant, which is between me and you and every living creature of all flesh; and the waters shall no more become a flood to destroy all flesh.

We've already discussed homosexuality as no worse than any other sin in God's eyes, but you are still flinging the flag of your sin in God's face, and it will bring Him down. The rainbow does not belong to the sin of man it belongs to God. Even more than that, it is the Shekinah glory, the very throne of God himself that you are seeing a glimpse of.

It is an abomination to the Lord to use that as a symbol for sin. I would never wave a flag at God of the sins that I've committed and I'm guessing you wouldn't either on purpose. That kind of symbolism is planted among us by the devil himself to offend our Lord. Waving the flag of the very promise of God that he won't destroy us for our sin. With a flag of PRIDE IN OUR SIN! Really?

Satan uses symbolism just like God does. He tries to copy everything God does.

Back to the trees in the Garden... We've discussed how God uses symbolism and parables. I think that is part of the beautiful way that the Holy Spirit uncovers things to your spirit. He calls things to your remembrance.

Now that we have established that there wasn't an apple tree in the garden. What were those two trees?

Well, the fig tree was satan. Those were the leaves that Adam and Eve covered up their privates with when God came looking for them. Prior to that they were not aware of their nakedness until satan "showed them".

Side note and weird fact on the fig tree itself. It does not flower, because it is actually an inverted flower. (Remember this for chapter 8 – Jesus, talking about the upside down) It is pollinated by a tiny type of wasp that penetrates the fruit to go in and pollinate all of the tiny flower seeds which are inside and then dies in there. Of course satan's tree is pollinated by a wasp that must die inside. Makes perfect sense...

Further biblical evidence that this was satan's tree. It was the fig tree that Jesus cursed, saying after Him that tree would not bear any more fruit.

Mark 11:13-14 And seeing a fig tree afar off having leaves, he came, if haply he might find any thing thereon: and when he came to it, he found nothing but leaves; for the time of figs was not yet. And Jesus answered and said unto it, No man eat fruit of thee hereafter for ever. And his disciples heard it.

Mark 11:20-22 And in the morning, as they passed by, they saw the fig tree dried up from the roots. And Peter calling to remembrance saith unto him, Master, behold, the fig tree which thou cursedst is withered away. And Jesus answering saith unto them, Have faith in God.

Jeremiah 29:17 Thus saith the Lord of hosts; Behold, I will send upon them the sword, the famine, and the pestilence, and will make them like vile figs, that cannot be eaten, they are so evil.

Many think the parable of the fig tree refers to Israel becoming a state which happened in 1948. I do think that is a marker, as God is gathering Israel back together. But, I don't think it is the subject of the parable of the fig tree. I think that fig tree was and has always been a parable for satan. And, Jesus was warning us.

Luke 21:29-31 And he spake to them a parable; Behold the fig tree, and all the trees; When they now shoot forth, ye see and know of your own selves that summer is now nigh at hand. So likewise ye, when ye see these things come to pass, know ye that the kingdom of God is nigh at hand.

There was another parable Jesus spoke about the devil's children, that I think is one of the most important in the bible to understand. I believe his children (the tares) are what Jesus is referring to that was planted along with the good wheat (God's children). When you see those tares grow up (little fig trees shoot forth) then know the evil ones are fully grown up now. Know that summer is now, and harvest season is coming for them. The kingdom of God is near.

The full text below with Jesus' interpretation thereof. He doesn't make you guess at anything.

Matthew 13:24-30 Another parable put he forth unto them, saying, The kingdom of heaven is likened unto a man which sowed good seed in his field: But while men slept, his enemy came and sowed tares among the wheat, and went his way. But when the blade was sprung up, and brought forth fruit, then appeared the tares also. So the servants of the householder came and said unto him, Sir, didst not thou sow good seed in thy field? from whence then hath it tares? He said unto them, An enemy hath done this. The servants said unto him, Wilt thou then that we go and gather them up? But he said, Nay; lest while ye gather up the tares, ye root up also the wheat with them. Let both grow together until the harvest: and in the time of harvest I will say to the reapers, Gather ye together first the tares, and bind them in bundles to burn them: but gather the wheat into my barn.

And then the disciples asked for Jesus to explain the parable to them. Take note, that the Father purposely said to let the tares mature fully to ensure that one of His own wasn't accidentally taken into the fire. He doesn't make mistakes and Jesus Himself said He had not lost one.

Matthew 13:37-43 He answered and said unto them, He that soweth the good seed is the Son of man; The field is the world; the good seed are the children of the kingdom; but the tares are the children of the wicked one; The enemy that sowed them is the devil; the harvest is the end of the world; and the reapers are the angels. As therefore the tares are gathered and burned in the fire; so shall it be in the end of this world. The Son of man shall send forth his angels, and they shall gather out of his kingdom all things that offend, and them which do iniquity; And shall cast them into a furnace of fire: there shall be wailing and gnashing of teeth. Then shall the righteous shine forth as the sun in the kingdom of their Father. Who hath ears to hear, let him hear.

Ok, so if Satan is the fig tree what tree is Jesus?

Of course, Jesus is the Olive Tree. The olive tree with the pure anointing oil as He is the anointed ONE!

John 15:5-8 I am the vine, ye are the branches: He that abideth in me, and I in him, the same bringeth forth much fruit: for without me ye can do nothing. If a man abide not in me, he is cast forth as a branch, and is withered; and men gather them, and cast them into the fire, and they are burned.

If ye abide in me, and my words abide in you, ye shall ask what ye will, and it shall be done unto you. Herein is my Father glorified, that ye bear much fruit; so shall ye be my disciples.

When I was in Israel, we learned about how olive oil is made. They told us that they had to crush the olives and that eighty percent of what came out of them was "black water". It struck me, that was like us. Eighty percent of what is in us is sin and corruptible.

We must be squeezed in this life to get rid of that black water. So that we have oil in our lamps for the wedding. You will learn all about this in the last chapter.

If we think about it in terms of our Lord and Savior, his body had to be crushed and take on all of the black water in that tree in order to have that unending oil of righteousness available to us. How precious it is…

Just as the serpent had to be raised up upon a cross so did Jesus. Both trees pulled up out of the ground and placed on it for the world.

John 3:14-15 And as Moses lifted up the serpent in the wilderness, even so must the Son of man be lifted up: That whosoever believeth in him should not perish, but have eternal life.

Israel was being bitten by serpents and dying when they came out of Egypt and were in the wilderness. Satan hates God's children. God told Moses to kill a serpent and put it on a cross and raise it up. Anyone who looked upon it would be healed.

Side bar: I still struggle with why this is our symbol of medicine. Trying to heal ourselves maybe? I'll leave that one to the Holy Spirit because He is still unveiling that one to me. I also had in my notes from Israel that they worshipped a Greek God called Asclepius for healing that had a rod with a serpent on it that could supposedly heal anything, even raise someone from the dead. He may have been able to heal but only God can give life.

As children of God, we look to Jesus on the cross for our healing. Mind, body and soul. Not to satan, who by the way is only healing the problems he created.

Much like the choice in the garden, we have a choice in our heart. If Jesus lives in you, where do you think the devil wants to be? You are the battleground dear ones. Always have been….

God's ultimate will is for ALL to come to repentance and to be with Him.

Matthew 18:11-13 For the Son of man is come to save that which was lost. How think ye? if a man have an hundred sheep, and one of them be gone astray, doth he not leave the ninety and nine, and goeth into the mountains, and seeketh that which is gone astray? And if so be that he find it, verily I say unto you, he rejoiceth more of that sheep, than of the ninety and nine which went not astray

The end will not come until the Word of God is sealed in our minds. And, the Word of God, Jesus, is the oil needed for the wedding in the last chapter of this book, Kosmos.

Revelation 7:2 And I saw another angel ascending from the east, having the seal of the living God: and he cried with a loud voice to the four angels, to whom it was given to hurt the earth and the sea, Saying, Hurt not the earth, neither the sea, nor the trees, till we have sealed the servants of our God in their foreheads.

Matthew 25:32-34 And before him shall be gathered all nations: and he shall separate them one from another, as a shepherd divideth his sheep from the goats: And he shall set the sheep on his right hand, but the goats on the left. Then shall the King say unto them on his right hand, Come, ye blessed of my Father, inherit the kingdom prepared for you from the foundation of the world:

Matthew 25:41 Then shall he say also unto them on the left hand, Depart from me, ye cursed, into everlasting fire, prepared for the devil and his angels:

Chapter 7

Gentleness

Death… Something we are all afraid of. I believe that fear is built into us for a reason. If we knew how wonderful heaven was, we would all want to off ourselves to get there sooner. I also believe that God is the gentlest in this process and uses it to draw us nearer to Him.

A very dear friend of mine who is a nun told me after my Father passed that God takes all souls at their most opportune time of salvation. I found that extremely profound and comforting. Somehow that made sense of everything to me. Every car accident, illness, tragedy… even involving children are blessings if you truly believe they are going home to be with their loving Father. We will of course grieve because we miss them in this life, but we will be reunited with them. I believe that with all of my heart because of these experiences.

Hardy was my grandfather and a tough old cowboy. I don't know why I didn't call him grandpa, I just always called him Hardy. Same with my grandmother, Dorothy. Hardy did a little bit of everything, but he always had horses and loved them. I remember riding when I was very young.

He was the first person that died in my life that I loved dearly. I was about 8 years old.

He had a stroke and was able to get around after, but he couldn't move one of his arms and couldn't chew anything. I can remember my mom putting entire steak dinners into a blender for him. As was her nature as a caretaker, she had brought him home to take care of him.

After the stroke, he would moan and call out for my mom (Flora Mae) all night which drove us all crazy. One night my mom completely lost it. My sister had just had a baby and was staying with us. He was being particularly loud and persistent with calling for her. My mom tried to quiet him several times to no avail.

My sister and I awoke to Hardy being tied up in a sheet on the recliner in the living room with a bandana in his mouth. My mom was giving it to him about how he was going to stay there all night if he couldn't be quiet because he was waking up the baby. She didn't tie it tight because his skin was thin, and she didn't want to hurt him. She just wanted him to quit yelling!

He immediately got loose and yelled in her face "Flora Mae". She really lost it then! My sister and I quickly announced that we were up and went down and helped calm the situation.

Later in my life I took care of both my father and mother after strokes. God used this experience to prepare me for taking care of them. He gave me peace about losing it on them sometimes. I knew and had learned that it was forgivable to lose your patience, and it happens to everyone…. He uses every little thing to teach us. Especially the hard stuff.

All of a sudden, a few months before Hardy died, he suddenly quit moaning and yelling for my mom. She asked him why and he told us that an angel had come to him and told him that God wasn't going to take him until he was ready. And, that he could be at peace and go to sleep and not worry. Turned out he was afraid to die. All of that moaning and yelling was to keep himself awake because he was afraid that he would die in his sleep. How gentle He is with us…

God was close to me when He took my father for a very long time because I think he knew how devastating it was going to be… not just on me but our whole family. My father had a personality that just filled up the room. He made everyone feel like they were his best friend whether you were a politician (which he was for most of his life) or the guy that changed his oil.

I remember at his funeral one of the biggest bouquets of flowers was from the Jiffy Lube where he had gotten oil changes for about forty years. I remember being struck that those flowers really summed up his character. That the guys that changed his oil loved him because he would talk to them and relate to them as a friend. He was their friend, and he was to everyone he met. I was so proud of that and proud to be his daughter.

My dad had gone to the Houston area to play in a golf tournament with my brother. I think I had just graduated college at the time. As they pulled up to the course, my father started having a heart attack. The golf course was fairly remote and thinking fast my brother just threw him back in the car and started driving back to Houston to the Methodist Hospital. That hospital was widely known as cutting edge when it came to their cardiac center.

There were two ways to get there, one of which involved a tunnel. My brother came to the stop light where he had to make a decision on which way to go. My dad was having trouble breathing at this point and my brother was panicking. Two older ladies walked up to the car, knocked on his window and asked him if he needed help.

I mean really when does this happen that two strangers knock on your window and ask if you need help. Much less old ladies. I truly believe they were angels sent by God.

He told them about dad and that he wasn't sure whether he should take the tunnel. They told him that he could, and it might be faster (which he knew) but often there were accidents in there and he could be stuck for hours, which dad would definitely not survive. So, they recommended that he go around, which he did.

Now there were a couple of miracles here.

When he got to the hospital, they immediately gave him a new shot that had just been approved by the FDA. There were literally only like three hospitals that had this available in the world. It was a new type of blood thinner which worked really fast and could buy someone having a heart attack some time. What are the odds that my father was playing in a golf tournament in Houston when he had his heart attack and has access to this kind of cutting-edge technology in cardiac care.

That evening we all got to the hospital from Austin and my brother was telling us his crazy story about the ladies and the tunnel. A nurse overheard this and asked if we had seen the news. Apparently, there was an accident in the tunnel at that time and my brother would have been stuck there for several hours. Later, the doctor confirmed that my dad had about 20 minutes to live when they arrived. Not only would he not have made it through the tunnel. But had he gone to any other hospital, he would have died because they didn't have access to that shot.

He had a successful surgery and was able to live another 20 years because of these miracles.

Fast forward about 20 years…

I had only been married about a year and was living in Dallas when my father had his stroke. It was horrible and catastrophic. He was basically in a coma for about a week.

During that time, we had to make a decision on whether or not to put a feeding tube in him to survive. He had not left any advance directives so we did not know what his wishes were and they were unable to tell us what his cognitive and physical ability would be if and when he woke up.

We asked our doctor what he would do… and he basically said that if it were his father he would give him the chance because there was a chance that he could mostly recover. So, we decided to do it.

I don't remember how long he was actually unconscious, but it seemed forever. Then one day the hospital called my mom and said he was awake and talking. We all rushed to the hospital immediately and it was a true miracle. He was wide awake! He recognized all of us and was so happy and talking and laughing. We couldn't believe it… the doctors couldn't believe it!

My sister asked him where he had been. He said he had been flying. "Flying where" she said? "Out there"… and he pointed towards the window. "With who," she said? He proceeded to name all five of his brothers and sisters that had already passed on and his mom and dad. He said it very matter of fact and was smiling from ear to ear. We were all crying with joy and completely amazed and in shock. It was truly beautiful…

He didn't give a whole lot of detail past that. We told him what had happened and how worried we had all been about him and all of the people that were praying for him. He seemed peaceful and happy and very thankful. (I just realized I'll fly away is playing in the background on radio as I write this…precious)

This only lasted a few hours… by that afternoon he couldn't really speak anymore and never would again. He could understand you and would nod and point but couldn't really talk or eat. Also, the stroke had left him with mobility in only one arm and he couldn't move either of his legs.

He went through rehabilitation at the hospital and then at another facility for a few months and then came home. He made some progress, but he was never able to overcome any of the handicaps the stroke had left him with.

I took care of him for a couple of months at home but realized quickly that I was not equipped for the twenty-four hour care by myself. We eventually put him in a nursing home and he lived over a year like that.

Had we known the hell that he would have to go through, we never would have agreed to the feeding tube. But I also believe as I said earlier, God takes each soul at their most opportune time of salvation, and I believe he still had some things to work out with God before he could go. Everything happens for a reason and as it should.

Towards the end he had been communicating to my brother that he wanted to go. I had the power of attorney and hadn't heard that from him and needed to know myself. I asked him, but to me he was mainly unresponsive at that time.

That night he ripped his own feeding tube out and threw it across the room. I got the message. It was pretty clear what his wishes were at that point.

They never put it back in and started to give him the morphine a few days later. Before that though, I was saying my goodbyes to him because they pretty much go into a coma after they begin the drugs. I was holding his hand and telling him how much I loved him when he glanced across the room.

His eyes got huge like a kid on Christmas morning that just suddenly got everything he wanted. He was squeezing my hand and had tears of joy. I couldn't see anything there. I asked him who it was. He just looked at me and smiled and shook his head like he couldn't tell me. I told him to go see them because he hadn't been that happy to see me in a year! And, I would see him soon enough…

I was outside when my brother called to say that his heart had just stopped. A deer had come up in the yard and wasn't ten feet from me. His heart started again, but I knew that deer was my dad or at least his spirit visiting me somehow. After his funeral, that same deer was in the backyard. I went and sat down on the grass, and he walked up to me and just stood there. Face to face for several minutes. It was precious and I knew a gift from God that everything was ok and he was at peace.

Closing on my dad… I believe God allowed him to talk to us in the hospital that day so that we would know where he was heading and where his soul was even when he was still trapped in this broken body on earth. Same for his vision right before his death. He was ecstatic to go where he was going. No fear anymore, just pure joy and happiness. His death was as gentle on us as it could be…

My mom was grace itself… so giving and loving. She was bedridden and wheelchair bound for many years before she passed away. That would have put most people in a pretty bad mood. But she was always cheerful and thankful. Fun-loving and sweet until the very end. Her body just sort of gave out.

She had been in the hospital for an infection that made her septic. She went through a couple of surgeries, but it quickly became evident after a few weeks in the hospital, this was it.

I remember after my sister and I told the doctor that we were going to stop treatment and bring her home, we went back into her hospital room. She had been kinda in and out of real consciousness for the last few days.

My sister picked up a bible and started reading from Psalms 23. The Lord is my Shepherd… and with those three words my mom sat up in bed and said loud and clear "I shall not want". With that little act we not only knew where she was going but how confident she was to get there. Again, peaceful and happy.

My mom's death was perfect. I know that sounds crazy to say but it was, and she deserved it.

We brought her home on a Thursday. She couldn't have solid food, but we could blend everything up for her. Everybody came out and started cooking all of her favorite things. She had a martini and a beer as were her favorites also.

Lots of coffee and sweets and lots of visits with family and friends. Everyone got to be with her and tell her how much they loved her and thank God she was conscious enough to say it back. Then Sunday after the last guest left, she just slipped off into heaven. It was a precious time… and as gentle as it could be.

I had two dogs during this time, Zen and Gigi. These dogs were my rock through all of this. I never had children, so these were my kids. I loved them and clung to them.

I was living in Florida after my mom passed for a few months. My niece (who is only six months younger than me) and also my best friend lives there with her family. So, I went there to be near them.

Zen had an episode while we were there and was diagnosed with what they call old dog syndrome. It looked like a stroke, but they say dogs don't have those.

I was still so broken from missing my mom that I couldn't imagine losing him too. I prayed and prayed for that dog, and he did make a pretty miraculous recovery. God granted my prayer and some more time with my sweet Zen.

The following year I was visiting my niece again in Florida for her son's graduation. Much of my family was there for the celebration. My ex-husband was taking care of my dogs for me. Zen got really sick again. And this time, he was beyond help and had to be put down.

I think God answered my prayer for more time with him, but also knew that I probably couldn't handle putting him down. So, he took that burden from me and also put me with the strength and support of my entire family when the time came. It was still tough, but it was a blessing how it all happened. As gentle as it could be….

I still can hardly talk about Gigi. We were connected. She also had a close call while I was in Florida (a different time for the holidays with my niece and family). She got pancreatitis and ended up in the hospital. I felt that I was losing her.

Again, I prayed and prayed for her too because I loved her but also, I was not ready to be by myself. I told God he was going to have to replace her after all of my loss if he took her from me. Also, that I knew that He had the power to save her, and I was claiming it. In the same breath I knew she had to go sometime, as we all do, and I would need his help coping if that was his will. Thankfully she made a miraculous recovery also and I got some more time with her. God answered my prayers again. How sweet and loving He is…

When the time came, He took her slow knowing that I couldn't take it all at once. She was sick for about a week and we tried everything to save her. The day before I had to put her down, He coordinated that my maid call me to come a few days early so the whole house would be clean for us to come home and spend the last night. It was right before Christmas so the maid coming early was a miracle in itself.

We got home that night to a clean house, and the internet and cable television were completely out. I don't believe in coincidences. I call them Godincidences. I know this was for us to spend sweet, focused time cuddling together in bed for one last night. It was precious time…

The next day my sweet doctor put me in a room with her. There was a candle, and it was quiet and relaxing. I fed her a chocolate chip cookie, which she had never had and loved, and then she was just sleeping in my arms. The doctor came in and knelt to give her the shots while she was sleeping. I had a sweet peace about it even though I was broken hearted.

Again, God put me in a situation where I couldn't just fall apart. I went home and had to cook and wrap presents because Christmas Eve was the next day. My entire family was coming to my house. Again, He made sure to surround me with family in my grief. He made it as gentle as He could…

A God Wink on these two… while I was living in Florida with them a major hurricane happened. Irma was gigantic and they ended up evacuating all of the Keys and Miami. Thankfully we got out just ahead of the crowds.

Long story short, we ended up in New Orleans to escape the storm. We were walking in Jackson Square and found a painting that is the spitting image of Zen and Gigi. You can see that painting below with a picture of the real-life Zen and Gigi so you can see how much they resemble it. People think I commissioned it, but I found it. And I knew it was a God wink for me, knowing I wouldn't have these guys forever. What a sweet and thoughtful present from my Father…

Even more amazing... I was in Port Aransas and a storm was coming. This was after both of their deaths. I was waiting for my brother and his wife to get there and was just hanging out on the porch.

I happened to turn around and look at the sky and there was Zen. It was not only visually him in the clouds, but I felt that overwhelming love. I just burst into tears and yelled out loud, "Oh Zen!" I couldn't believe it... I then remembered that I had my phone with me, so I took a picture. That is below with another shot of him for comparison.

    Then, a few minutes later after that cloud started to dissipate and here comes Gigi with those unmistakable ears of hers! How precious of Him to show me that they were in Heaven with Him. That they were happy and whole and playing on the clouds.

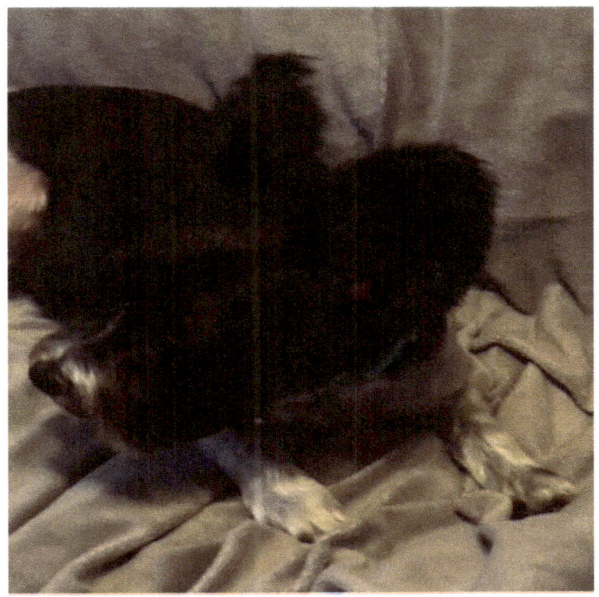

I have no doubt, especially for you animal lovers, that He wanted me to show you this too. These beautiful signs so that you would know where your fur babies are. That rainbow bridge is fur real!

AND, even more amazing still… I didn't see this till another friend brought it to my attention. But in the Jesus photo that is on the cover, you will notice that He is holding a dog. You guys, that is Gigi with those ears and exactly where and how I was holding her when she went to sleep. Now I know she left my arms and went to sleep in Jesus' arms. How precious and gentle He is… What a gift.

Chapter 8

Jesus

Philippians 2:9-11 Wherefore God also hath highly exalted him, and given him a name which is above every name: That at the name of Jesus every knee should bow, of things in heaven, and things in earth, and things under the earth; And that every tongue should confess that Jesus Christ is Lord, to the glory of God the Father.

Jesus being chapter eight just sort of happened. But it is a divine number, as that is the number for Jesus. Adam, who was at the top of Jesus' lineage on earth, was created on the eighth day.

Most people think the bible states that Adam and Eve created everyone, but that is not what it says. Everybody (all the gentiles and nations) was created on the sixth day. God rested on the seventh. (Each day is a thousand years don't forget according to Peter).

I'm guessing the kids were probably up to no good while God was resting. It doesn't really say that, but it makes sense. Because he comes back on the eighth day and realizes that we will need a Savior. So, He put a new plan in action and created Adam and Eve on the eighth day. Jesus our Savior would come through that bloodline.

They call this the Key of David because He was in that bloodline too. I'm not going to put all of that genealogy in here, but you can read it all the way from Adam to Jesus in Luke 3. And guess who the 8th person in that lineage was. Our righteous friend who built the ark, Noah.

Peter 2: 4-5 For if God spared not the angels that sinned, but cast them down to hell, and delivered them into chains of darkness, to be reserved unto judgment; And spared not the old world, but saved Noah the eighth person, a preacher of righteousness, bringing in the flood upon the world of the ungodly;

Pretty much the whole bible is about Jesus. It provides us information about His family history, the prophecy of His coming, His teaching while with us and His return.

Even the story of the Exodus from Egypt is about Jesus. When God warned them through Moses that He would take their first born of everything including their children, the Israelites were instructed to kill a lamb and put the blood around the door. In this manner, the death angel knew to pass over. This is the story that the Jews celebrate on Passover.

Ultimately it became Christ's blood that covers us. He was the Passover lamb for one and all times that causes the death angel to pass over us. The Lamb of God.

I did not realize until I went there that the Passover lambs used in Jerusalem were raised in Bethlehem. Of course, that had to be where He was born. The crucifixion itself took place at 3pm, which was the normal time for the afternoon sacrifice at the temple. There are so many details and beautiful things that He weaves together.

I had been following the 700 club for a while and was a contributor. One day, I received an email from them stating that they were going to be doing a tour of Israel for the 75th anniversary of Israel becoming a state. I immediately felt a burning in my chest and the Holy Spirit.

He communicates to all of us differently… I remember feeling sad in church sometimes because He had never "talked" to me. The only thing that was ever verbal (as we know it) to me was that night in bed when He said to read about me and you won't be afraid. The rest has been literally thoughts while praying that He puts in my mind and that burning in my chest, spirit. That's when I know… I explain that because I've had friends say longingly that they have never felt that. But I put to you, if you ask Him to show you, in your naked soul self, earnestly wanting to know Him. He will show Himself to you… I promise because He promised!

Jeremiah 29:13 And ye shall seek me, and find me, when ye shall search for me with all your heart.

Back to our story… I knew that I had to go on that trip. I still didn't sign up immediately though because I am stubborn.

Ezekiel 2:4 For they are impudent children and stiffhearted.

The next day… a friend of mine from high school reached out to me from Jordan. I had not heard from him in thirty years, so this was definitely a sign. There was multiple more in the coming days but needless to say, I finally booked the trip.

God had been preparing me in ways that I didn't even realize. He works that way… My church was starting a fast and I decided to do it with them. I'm not sure if I had ever fasted completely before, but I did this time. The day before I started that fast by the way was when I saw the evil one in what was my church at the time. That is covered more in Chapter 14 – The Church.

I started fasting the next day and met one of my friends from Tres Dias for coffee (just black in case you were wondering because of the fast). Tres Dias is an incredible organization that runs a Christian camp. It is a beautiful place for sanctification at all levels. I work at the camps a few times a year and I always meet Him there in wonderful ways.

Anyway, God had put in my heart recently that I had never confessed my sins to anyone else besides Him. I had repented to Him but not given breath to it. We are instructed to do so...

James 5:16 Confess your faults one to another, and pray one for another, that ye may be healed. The effectual fervent prayer of a righteous man availeth much.

So, I told her all of the worst things that I had ever done. God really gave me a soul sister in this friend. She calls me her garden friend. As in when Jesus took Peter, James and John with Him to pray in the Garden of Gethsemane before He was taken. Precious. She is so full of mercy and love. I know Christ put her in my life for such a time as this. She said the Lord had told her to say Aaron's blessing over me.

Numbers 6:24-27 The Lord bless thee, and keep thee: The Lord make his face shine upon thee, and be gracious unto thee: The Lord lift up his countenance upon thee, and give thee peace. And they shall put my name upon the children of Israel, and I will bless them.

Within that blessing you have the full Godhead. The Father bless you, Jesus shine His face upon you and the Holy Spirit give you peace. The Hebrew letter Yod is the beginning of each of those blessings and also is the first letter of the Divine Name of our Father YHVH and Yeshuah. Even the "Y" itself is the three in one. How precious all the meticulous details.

I didn't put all of this together at the time how this was preparing me for this journey. The devil sighting, the prayer and fasting, the confession and the blessing over me. He has you right where He wants you whether you know it or not.

A couple of days later, she sent me a scripture about being refined into gold. A metaphor of the sin or dross being burned off of us. What she didn't know, was that I had seen myself in her eyes with fire around me. It freaked me out and I didn't know quite how to verbalize that one. But after she sent me that scripture, I told her and that I thought it was the Holy Spirit in her cleansing me. She even had a gold countenance about her face. How beautiful it all is.

Zechariah 13:9 And I will bring the third part through the fire, and will refine them as silver is refined, and will try them as gold is tried: they shall call on my name, and I will hear them: I will say, It is my people: and they shall say, The Lord is my God.

I also believe this was the Holy Spirit baptizing me with fire as I had brought up earlier.

After all of that preparation, unbeknownst to me, I headed off on the trip!

One of the first places we visited was Nazareth, where Jesus grew up. We were on the street, and I noticed a man looking at me. He began to say a few words over me and then made a cross symbol in the air and then kissed the air. He then walked over to us and commented on what a beautiful bible I had in my hands. Which wasn't a bible at all but my journal.

He asked us what we were, to which we replied Christian. He said that was good and he was also, and that we needed to pray for the Christians in Nazareth. He said there weren't many, and they needed our prayers for them.

I don't pretend to understand what that was, but I know all of this was preparation for my baptism in the Jordan and ultimately the experience up on the temple mount and the Mount of Olives.

I was baptized when I was younger. But as a fifty+ adult to rededicate yourself, after all of the filthiness of living and to be washed clean again, was beauty. There were about twelve of us and those will forever be very special brothers and sisters to me. (You know who you are, and I love you!)

The baptism was important also because I believe it was another step in my cleansing to be in His presence. My garden friend, who I mentioned earlier, even set her alarm and got up to pray for me the whole time while I was being baptized. Now that's a friend.

After the baptism, we went up to Almagor which literally means "without fear". It overlooks the sea of Galilee and is a very special place. You can literally see where much of Jesus ministry had been accomplished. You could actually feel the peace in the air.

On the way up there, we saw these fields of yellow that were amazing! As far as the eye could see… We asked what they were and just guess. Mustard.

Matthew 17:20 And Jesus said unto them, Because of your unbelief: for verily I say unto you, If ye have faith as a grain of mustard seed, ye shall say unto this mountain, Remove hence to yonder place; and it shall remove; and nothing shall be impossible unto you.

After the tour (which was amazing!), I remained in Jerusalem for a week by myself. I kept trying to go to the temple mount, but it was always closed. This is Solomon's temple. It is also the same place where God asked Abraham to sacrifice his son and ultimately substituted a ram. (but didn't withhold his own Son from sacrificing)

It is now called the dome of the rock and is muslim. Because of their prayer calls throughout the day, it is often closed. And sometimes they just don't reopen it. Prayer by someone who is not muslim is forbidden.

On my third attempt, I was finally able to get up there. It was beautiful. You can see all of old and new Jerusalem to the west and the Kidron Valley and the Mount of Olives to the east.

As I was going through security, they took my journal with a cross on it thinking that it was a bible. They allowed it after I showed them that it was just my handwritten notes. I think they know exactly how powerful Christian's prayers are at that place.

Once up there, there was a beautiful cloud over the mosque. It was strange because it was low and the only cloud in the sky.

I walked over to the edge of the side opposite the Mount of Olives and began to pray… they were NOT going to stop me from praying. I felt the Spirit encouraging me to say the Lord's Prayer. So, I did. Out loud. I even filmed myself doing it and describing as in the scripture where His feet will hit the Mount of Olives and split it wide open.

Zechariah 14:4 And his feet shall stand in that day upon the mount of Olives, which is before Jerusalem on the east, and the mount of Olives shall cleave in the midst thereof toward the east and toward the west, and there shall be a very great valley;

I later thought, I was pretty crazy to do that… Being in a foreign country by myself and all. But when he puts on your heart to do something, you have to do it. Even if you don't understand why you are doing it. (Which is usually the case…)

After that, I went through the east gate (Damascus gate) to where the best guess of where Christ's tomb was. I really had no feeling of His presence there and as a matter of fact, a strong message in my soul of… I haven't been here since I arose. So I left…

I had been to the Mount of Olives on our tour, but the church up there had been closed for services when we were there. I was drawn to that place right then and wanted to see the inside of it. The church is called Dominus Flavit and it is shaped like a tear drop. It represents Jesus weeping over Jerusalem and praying for His people.

It was a lot easier getting up there by bus! I don't know how long it took me to climb up, but it was a while, and it was hot and uphill. When I got to the top, I entered the garden and there was a man there that appeared behind me and asked if I was ok. I said yes and then he jokingly asked if I wanted some coffee? No, I think I'm good, I said laughing! I told him that I had been there the other day and wanted to go into the church. He said there were services going on, but they were about done and I could wait. So, I went over to admire the view and pray.

I don't remember what I prayed about, but I do remember feeling peaceful and thankful for everything that I had experienced. The church let out and I went in and there was my friend again. Cleaning up after the service. He was moving chairs and I was just taking everything in. The view of Jerusalem was incredible behind the altar. The altar itself had a picture of a hen with all of her little chicks around her.

Luke 13:34 *O Jerusalem, Jerusalem, which killest the prophets, and stonest them that are sent unto thee; how often would I have gathered thy children together, as a hen doth gather her brood under her wings, and ye would not!*

He asked if I wanted my picture taken, and I said sure. We then just started talking about where I was from and what I was doing there. We walked outside and he picked out a postcard and gave it to me to remember. This was the scripture inside…

Luke 19:41-44 And when he was come near, he beheld the city, and wept over it, Saying, If thou hadst known, even thou, at least in this thy day, the things which belong unto thy peace! but now they are hid from thine eyes. For the days shall come upon thee, that thine enemies shall cast a trench about thee, and compass thee round, and keep thee in on every side, And shall lay thee even with the ground, and thy children within thee; and they shall not leave in thee one stone upon another; because thou knewest not the time of thy visitation.

We continued walking outside and the first tree we came to was a Spina Christi. He explained that most people think of the thorns in Jesus' crown as being from a rose. But it was actually from this tree. They were about 2-3 inches long and like a nail, they were so hard. It made me want to cry to even think about it. Here is the actual tree…

    I spent about thirty minutes with him just talking about that place and learning. Afterwards, He took my arm in his and walked me out. His name was David.

    As I was leaving the garden around the church, I looked up in the sky and it seemed crazy looking to me, for lack of a better term. It was dark but then bright around the sun. I just started taking pictures as I do...

It wasn't until I got home that I saw the image in those pictures as I was going through them about two months later. At first, it looked to me like someone sitting on top of the sun. I have an online ministry on Facebook called Prayforme so I posted it there. I thought that picture in itself was cool and might inspire someone's faith.

Then, someone told me to turn it upside down in one of the comments. That is the image that you see on the cover of this book. That is the face of Jesus Christ, the Anointed One, our Lord and Savior, King of Kings and Lord of Lords.

Revelation 1:7 Behold, he cometh with clouds; and every eye shall see him, and they also which pierced him: and all kindreds of the earth shall wail because of him.

Revelation 14:14 And I looked, and behold a white cloud, and upon the cloud one sat like unto the Son of man, having on his head a golden crown, and in his hand a sharp sickle.

I have no idea why He allowed me to take that picture. But I think it has to do with my being obedient to the Spirit in saying the Lord's prayer on the temple mount. And, that is probably why they were so worried about anyone praying up there.

Here is the Lord's prayer in case you don't know it or even if you do. Read these words expectantly with God in the clouds above you. Because He is.

Matthew 6:9-13 After this manner therefore pray ye: Our Father which art in heaven, Hallowed be thy name. Thy kingdom come, Thy will be done in earth, as it is in heaven. Give us this day our daily bread. And forgive us our debts, as we forgive our debtors. And lead us not into temptation, but deliver us from evil: For thine is the kingdom, and the power, and the glory, for ever. Amen.

I prayed it with faith and belief that it will happen and look at what happened. I know it sounds crazy, but He is coming in the clouds, and He is coming soon.

Even crazier, way back in Isaiah he talked about things being upside down.

Isaiah 29:13-16 Wherefore the Lord said, Forasmuch as this people draw near me with their mouth, and with their lips do honour me, but have removed their heart far from me, and their fear toward me is taught by the precept of men: Therefore, behold, I will proceed to do a marvellous work among this people, even a marvellous work and a wonder: for the wisdom of their wise men shall perish, and the understanding of their prudent men shall be hid. Woe unto them that seek deep to hide their counsel from the Lord, and their works are in the dark, and they say, Who seeth us? and who knoweth us? Surely your turning of things upside down shall be esteemed as the potter's clay: for shall the work say of him that made it, He made me not? or shall the thing framed say of him that framed it, He had no understanding?

I was supposed to be born a boy or a girl. God made a mistake. I don't think so dear ones... The clay doesn't talk back and question the potter that made it.

I had another experience a little over a year later. I was in Athens and had just wandered out to do some shopping before dinner with the group that I was with. There was a cart selling something right at the entrance to the shopping street. Sitting behind it was a homeless man wearing a white long gown type of thing. Upon reflection it was sort of shimmering... He was sort of shimmering. But your eyes can't process or believe things sometimes when you see them.

Luke 24:15-16 And it came to pass, that, while they communed together and reasoned, Jesus himself drew near, and went with them. But their eyes were holden that they should not know him.

He had his arms crossed over his legs with his head on top of them. He was shivering and with a shaky voice he said, "help me, help me, living on the street is killing me". I silently started praying for this man for God to heal him and help him. I almost started to walk away and then something pulled me back.

The voice sounded familiar and almost like someone was faking it or throwing their voice. I decided to give him a couple of euros and a little Jesus figurine that I had been handing out to people. (Look them up they are a wonderful, simple way to spread the love of God)

As I approached him, he was picking at the sores on his arm that actually went all the way through. I could see bone and the pavement through the center of his arms. I extended my hand with the euros and the little Jesus and said "Sir". With that he started to look up with a big smile and I simply said, "He loves you" and handed him those two things and walked away abruptly.

Later, upon reflection, I realized who it was. Because that big smile was one of pride in me. His daughter. You really do never know when you extend a kindness, that you may be actually doing it to Jesus.

Matthew 17:2 And was transfigured before them: and his face did shine as the sun, and his raiment was white as the light.

Matthew 25:40 And the King shall answer and say unto them, Verily I say unto you, Inasmuch as ye have done it unto one of the least of these my brethren, ye have done it unto me.

We have the same choice that there was in the beginning. The choice of Life or death. The Tree of Life or the tree of the knowledge of good and evil. The Olive Tree or the fig tree. Jesus or satan.

Romans 5:1-2 Therefore being justified by faith, we have peace with God through our Lord Jesus Christ: By whom also we have access by faith into this grace wherein we stand, and rejoice in hope of the glory of God.

Revelation 1:8 I am Alpha and Omega, the beginning and the ending, saith the Lord, which is, and which was, and which is to come, the Almighty.

Chapter 9

The Enemy

Who is the devil?

Ezekiel 28:12-19 Son of man, take up a lamentation upon the king of Tyrus, and say unto him, Thus saith the Lord God; Thou sealest up the sum, full of wisdom, and perfect in beauty. Thou hast been in Eden the garden of God; every precious stone was thy covering, the sardius, topaz, and the diamond, the beryl, the onyx, and the jasper, the sapphire, the emerald, and the carbuncle, and gold: the workmanship of thy tabrets and of thy pipes was prepared in thee in the day that thou wast created. Thou art the anointed cherub that covereth; and I have set thee so: thou wast upon the holy mountain of God; thou hast walked up and down in the midst of the stones of fire. Thou wast perfect in thy ways from the day that thou wast created, till iniquity was found in thee. By the multitude of thy merchandise they have filled the midst of thee with violence, and thou hast sinned: therefore I will cast thee as profane out of the mountain of God: and I will destroy thee, O covering cherub, from the midst of the stones of fire. Thine heart was lifted up because of thy beauty, thou hast corrupted thy wisdom by reason of thy brightness: I will cast thee to the ground, I will lay thee before kings, that they may behold thee. Thou hast defiled thy sanctuaries by the multitude of thine iniquities, by the iniquity of thy traffick; therefore will I bring forth a fire from the midst of thee, it shall devour thee, and I will bring thee to ashes upon the earth in the sight of all them that behold thee. All they that know thee among the people shall be astonished at thee: thou shalt be a terror, and never shalt thou be any more.

He is called many things in the bible. However, God never reveals his original name. I believe that is because he was completely stripped of that title to never be referred to in such a holy manner again. The closest to describing him in his original estate with God was lucifer or heylel which means the shining one. He will come pretending to be the Daystar (Jesus Christ) as the "morning star".

He is also known as the King of Tyrus or Tyre, as in the scripture from Ezekiel above. Tyre means rock, and again he is pretending to be our rock, which there is only one, Jesus Christ. Our rock of salvation, the true cornerstone. Tyre controlled all of the merchant ships and therefore the distribution channel for all of the goods. (Reminds you of Amazon today doesn't it) Through the ports of Tyre went all of the merchant ships of "Tarshish". I believe this could be where the devil will be kicked back out onto earth, as it is prophesied (and may already be here) and described in Chapter 15 – The Anti-Christ.

Isaiah 23:1 The burden of Tyre. Howl, ye ships of Tarshish; for it is laid waste, so that there is no house, no entering in: from the land of Chittim it is revealed to them.

Isaiah 23:5-8 As at the report concerning Egypt, so shall they be sorely pained at the report of Tyre. Pass ye over to Tarshish; howl, ye inhabitants of the isle. Is this your joyous city, whose antiquity is of ancient days? her own feet shall carry her afar off to sojourn. Who hath taken this counsel against Tyre, the crowning city, whose merchants are princes, whose traffickers are the honourable of the earth?

Isaiah 23:11 He stretched out his hand over the sea, he shook the kingdoms: the Lord hath given a commandment against the merchant city, to destroy the strong holds thereof.

I've scoured scripture and I don't really find where it says the full reason God destroyed the first earth age. Many preachers quote Revelation 12 below as stating that satan deceived a third of God's children, which is why He destroyed it. But that verse says he drew the stars from heaven down to earth, so that doesn't really make sense to me.

Revelation 12:4 And his tail drew the third part of the stars of heaven, and did cast them to the earth:

I do believe it was satan's pride and likely to do with Tyre. Good chance it was something he did to make himself like God. Just not sure what exactly that was and really, why would we have any record of that when God completely destroyed that world age. I think that is just one of those that we won't know until we get to Heaven. And, I doubt we will care by then anyway.

Satan literally means the adversary in just about every biblical language you can think of... and that is what he is.

The name devil literally means slanderer. Similarly, he is also known as the accuser in front of our Holy Father.

Revelation 12:10 for the accuser of our brethren is cast down, which accused them before our God day and night.

He is called beelzebul (Lord of the Dung Hill) and beelzebub (Lord of the Flies), which the name baal is derived from meaning lord. He is also called azazel, the serpent and the dragon.

We talked about how he caused the destruction of the first earth age. Let's talk about this one.

The very first prophecy in the Bible is regarding satan, which was God's judgement on him after deceiving Eve and causing the fall of this world age into sin.

Genesis 3:15 And I will put enmity between thee and the woman, and between thy seed and her seed; it shall bruise thy head, and thou shalt bruise his heel.

God is so loving... He could have destroyed the world again, but His will is for all to come to repentance. Even the tares if they will accept Jesus. Nothing says they can't.

Ezekiel 33:11 Say unto them, As I live, saith the Lord God, I have no pleasure in the death of the wicked; but that the wicked turn from his way and live: turn ye, turn ye from your evil ways; for why will ye die, O house of Israel?

The devil, however, is already judged according to that prophecy in Genesis. The first part was fulfilled when they crucified Christ and "bruised his heel", that act sealed his fate. Satan's head will be "bruised" before this is all over.

Ephesians 2:15-16 Having abolished in his flesh the enmity, even the law of commandments contained in ordinances; for to make in himself of twain one new man, so making peace; And that he might reconcile both unto God in one body by the cross, having slain the enmity thereby:

Satan was not alone in all of this. There were fallen angels that came down with him to corrupt man. Peter talked about their punishment and their current habitation in this earth.

2 Peter 2:4-9 For if God spared not the angels that sinned, but cast them down to hell, and delivered them into chains of darkness, to be reserved unto judgment; And spared not the old world, but saved Noah the eighth person, a preacher of righteousness, bringing in the flood upon the world of the ungodly; And turning the cities of Sodom and Gomorrha into ashes condemned them with an overthrow, making them an ensample unto those that after should live ungodly; And delivered just Lot, vexed with the filthy conversation of the wicked: (For that righteous man dwelling among them, in seeing and hearing, vexed his righteous soul from day to day with their unlawful deeds;) The Lord knoweth how to deliver the godly out of temptations, and to reserve the unjust unto the day of judgment to be punished:

The word hell used in that verse is "tartarus" in the Greek, which is a different term than is normally used in the bible for hell. It's actually a term from Greek mythology for the very inner part of the underworld where gods locked up their enemies. Very interesting that he would use that term for the fallen angels. But actually, they are our enemies so it would be a term that they would have fully understood back then. And all the implications thereof…

This is also talked about in Jude.

Jude 1:6 And the angels which kept not their first estate, but left their own habitation, he hath reserved in everlasting chains under darkness unto the judgment of the great day.

Reference to the fallen angel's banishment can also be found in the Old Testament.

Psalms 74:20 Have respect unto the covenant: for the dark places of the earth are full of the habitations of cruelty.

God is warning to respect his covenant because you don't want to end up down there with them.

I keep having these visions of ants or bodies, all crawling over each other trying to reach a far-off light. This vision is persistent. Like for years I've had it... and while writing this book almost daily. Could have something to do with these fallen angels chained up in the dark places of the earth.

There has also been one verse that I couldn't understand where God wanted me to put it, but it was clear that He wanted it in here.

Acts 14:2 But the unbelieving Jews stirred up the Gentiles, and made their minds evil affected against the brethren.

Those "unbelieving jews" aren't our brothers and sisters of Judah. They are the spirits of the fallen angels that have the power to vex us and make our minds evil against good things. And, unfortunately, against each other. But that is almost over.

God knows who to blame for all of the sin in this world. Not that we have no responsibility in our sin. We always have to repent for what we've done. But, I think God ultimately holds satan and not us responsible for everything that has ever happened bad on this planet. He and his angels were the ones that taught us how to be bad. And still do through those spirits. We didn't naturally have that tendency because God's creation is always perfect.

Those same spirits are now teaching our children that they can choose their gender and change through surgery, everything about their bodies. That is basically convincing them that they are their own gods. What do you think they are doing creating their own virtual realities online? Literally creating their own "worlds". Very lonely and isolated worlds with only you know who whispering to them about their "creations".

Man has been trying to make their own path to "enlightenment", or God, since we came into existence. This path to "enlightenment" can be evidenced in many religions and many ceremonies with magic and drugs all taught by our evil friends. Folks, throughout human history, whenever we have tried to make a human king for ourselves or a God or get to heaven or "reach enlightenment", all of those paths have led to hell. Either hell on earth or hell to come. There is nothing new under the sun and that deception is all orchestrated by the same jerk.

The prophecy of what is coming to him and his buddies at the end of this age can be found in Isaiah.

Isaiah 14:12-22 How art thou fallen from heaven, O Lucifer, son of the morning! how art thou cut down to the ground, which didst weaken the nations! For thou hast said in thine heart, I will ascend into heaven, I will exalt my throne above the stars of God: I will sit also upon the mount of the congregation, in the sides of the north: I will ascend above the heights of the clouds; I will be like the most High. Yet thou shalt be brought down to hell, to the sides of the pit. They that see thee shall narrowly look upon thee, and consider thee, saying, Is this the man that made the earth to tremble, that did shake kingdoms; That made the world as a wilderness, and destroyed the cities thereof; that opened not the house of his prisoners? All the kings of the nations, even all of them, lie in glory, every one in his own house. But thou art cast out of thy grave like an abominable branch, and as the raiment of those that are slain, thrust through with a sword, that go down to the stones of the pit; as a carcase trodden under feet. Thou shalt not be joined with them in burial, because thou hast destroyed thy land, and slain thy people: the seed of evildoers shall never be renowned. Prepare slaughter for his children for the iniquity of their fathers; that they do not rise, nor possess the land, nor fill the face of the world with cities. For I will rise up against them, saith the Lord of hosts, and cut off from Babylon the name, and remnant, and son, and nephew, saith the Lord.

He has but a short time and his end has already been proclaimed and promised by our Lord. Hallelujah!

Chapter 10

The Eye

2 Chronicles 16:9 For the eyes of the Lord run to and fro throughout the whole earth, to shew himself strong in the behalf of them whose heart is perfect toward him.

This kind of verse used to freak me out a little bit to be honest. It just sounds scary… But since seeing Jesus in the sun a couple of years ago, that has opened my mind a bit. And, my eyes. He is part of the sun or rather sits on top of it in this world. And upside down (or right side up depending on how you look at it), is over heaven and able to see all that is happening.

Psalms 34:15 The eyes of the Lord are upon the righteous, and his ears are open unto their cry.

Matthew 6:22-23 The light of the body is the eye: if therefore thine eye be single, thy whole body shall be full of light. But if thine eye be evil, thy whole body shall be full of darkness. If therefore the light that is in thee be darkness, how great is that darkness!

This goes back to Peter trying to walk on the water with Jesus. As long as he was looking at Jesus, he could stand on the water with Him. But as soon as he took his eyes off of Him, he began to sink. If you are living with your spiritual eyes open and on Jesus, the waters of this world will not overtake you.

I began seeing visions of an eye staring back at me a few years ago. It was scary at first, but I eventually got used to it. Now, I know that it is the Holy Spirit guiding me. When I don't see it, I know that I have drifted and taken my eyes off Jesus.

Psalm 32:8 I will instruct thee and teach thee in the way which thou shalt go: I will guide thee with mine eye.

I've prayed whether to share any of this, because I know how it sounds. But, He wanted me too. Maybe some of you have experienced this as well. I doubt I am the only one.

While I was traveling in Greece, they have the "evil eye" everywhere. It is supposedly a curse from Greek culture passed down many generations. Amulets with it have been found dated over 5,000 years ago. It was believed that if someone was jealous of you, they could curse you with an evil glare. At least, that is what is on the internet now when you look it up.

I remember getting one of these from a friend in my twenties (long time ago), and it was supposed to protect you from evil spirits. That definition is no longer out there. Friends, the internet is wonderful but think how easy it is to manipulate all of the information out there! They can literally rewrite everything.

After the Jesus photo needing to be turned upside down to see Him properly, it started me thinking that this world is indeed upside down. Pretty much everything that is considered good is probably bad and vice versa. Isaiah even prophesied about this.

Isaiah 5:20 Woe unto them that call evil good, and good evil; that put darkness for light, and light for darkness; that put bitter for sweet, and sweet for bitter!

Now this eye, that is supposedly "evil" … Could this be God's protective eye over us? Makes sense…

On the same trip, I was in Pompeii and there were penises over many of the doors there. Yep, you heard me right. I asked our tour guide what those were for and he said that they were against the evil eye. Hmmmm… That would make sense that satan would try to use a penis, symbolic of his perversion in fornication, to combat God. Also makes sense with what happened there.

Asherah or ashtoreth (asherim is plural) was a pagan fertility goddess and the wooden cult object created to represent her. They would erect this pole which was a phallic symbol and worship around it in the groves in ceremonies associated with baal (one of satan's names). Many references to this have been removed from the Bible in the newer translations.

There are symbols of these literally everywhere! Practically every cathedral in Italy has an obelisk in front of it which is just the Egyptian version of the asherah pole. Why are these put in front of the cathedrals? Think about how offensive that is to God.

We also have them in America everywhere. They are all over the graveyards. What do you think the Washington monument is?

I had a disturbing encounter in the garden right before the Vatican even of an "eye". Which, by the way, also has a giant obelisk, asherah or whatever you want to call it, in front of it in St. Peter's Square. Here is a picture of that eye. That protective sweet eye of God following us… portrayed as broken and deformed, evil.

    I don't really know what else to say about that, I think a picture speaks a thousand words.

    I have had personal experience with the spiritual manifestation of the penis side of things as well… It was Thanksgiving and a weird one. Much of my family was out of town and the ones who weren't, were all the way in another city and there was a bad storm. We weren't going to have dinner till that night and that would have had me driving late in the worst of the storm. I decided just to skip it (which I will never do again) and hang out at the house.

    As I do sometimes, I had a little too much wine. I was probably feeling sorry for myself, spending Thanksgiving alone. (although I made that choice) I turned over in bed and happened to glance at the doorway. There was something. I don't know if it was a devil or spirit or what, but it had a giant penis. I must have recognized him in my spirit because I wasn't afraid. I simply turned over and said Lord, get this guy away from me. When I turned back over, he was gone.

It wasn't a man, and it was really short... It almost looked like a green under armour figure with a giant penis. I know this sounds crazy, but it happened. I can't fully explain it to you because I don't completely understand it myself. My hope is that some of you have had similar experiences, and we can give breath to this evil to dispel it.

A note about my spiritual state to have allowed this. Satan and his demons prey on loneliness. The devil wants nothing more than to keep you separated from family and friends to control your mind and spirit. He's like an abusive husband.

I don't think there is anything wrong with drinking. But the bible tells us to not be drunk. I cannot cast a stone at that one for sure. Pretty much my whole family has struggled with that at one time or another. But I do know that being drunk gives the devil a foot hold in your mind. They don't call alcohol spirits for nothing.

Now satan tries to copy everything God does because he wants to be God. I had another experience with an eye, but it was satan in this vision.

This time I was lying in bed and the eye that I described earlier appeared, but it was different. It almost looked like the eye of a reptile staring back at me. But it seemed like it was inside of me like the good eye. This is how good he is at deceiving us.

I started praying and saying silently, "I know that if this is coming from inside me that it is you Lord. So please give me peace, because this is a little scary". It kept staring at me... I then said out loud, "if this is not from you then I rebuke whoever this is in your name, in JESUS name!". And with that it withdrew slowly.

The devil is supernatural and powerful. He can put you in a state of wonder or trance that you are not sure what is real and what is not. But he cannot read your thoughts, and God can get rid of him, no problem. Always know that you have that power in Jesus' name too!

Luke 10:19 Behold, I give unto you power to tread on serpents and scorpions, and over all the power of the enemy: and nothing shall by any means hurt you.

Chapter 11

The Flood

This chapter isn't about Noah's Flood, but my flood.

We lived on a golf course, that had a creek running beside it, for pretty much my whole life. We moved out there when I was about seven years old. The house was on a huge hill with a big yard before you came to the golf course. It was probably a good four or five hundred yards to the creek.

It was a wonderful home with plenty of room for my large family. And as often was the case, anyone of our friends who happened to be down on their luck or just needed some family time. It was always full of people and fun!

It changed of course over the years and especially after my dad passed. My mom, that same year became bedbound, and I had to have full time help living with me to help take care of her.

The creek would periodically flood out of the banks. It would flood the golf course and every few years may come a little bit up the hill, but as I said… It was a big hill.

One night, my neighbor started knocking and ringing my doorbell about five in the morning frantically. I awoke and opened the door, only after realizing who it was, and he told me that we needed to think about getting out. He said the creek was up… I thanked him and shut the door not really taking it too seriously. Because as I said… It was a big hill.

I went to the back door and was shocked that when I opened it, the water was already over that big hill and almost to the back porch. I slammed the door and yelled for my caregiver to help me with my Mom.

She got her ready to get in the car, which was a Nissan Pathfinder. (This will be important later) I proceeded to grab photo albums, my home insurance file and my dogs. We all loaded up in the car and began to drive out of the neighborhood.

There was only one road in and out of where we lived, and it curved around with the golf course and next to the creek. When I got to the last part of the road before it went up a hill, there was a cop car that passed me. He gave me two fingers to go ahead and pass. There was some water on the road at that point, but not much. I'm sure he thought it was safe since he had just crossed that road, and I was in a higher pathfinder. I also saw in the distance a fire truck, so they were likely about to shut the road down.

Literally, a few seconds later the water was OVER the hood of my car. They later said the force of that water was more than the force of Niagara Falls. I felt the car leave the pavement and I knew we were probably dead.

I began to scream pray. I don't know if you've ever done it, but you would know if you had. Through tears, I was screaming and begging God to please just let us pass. Please! Then scripture started coming to my mind and I started quoting back to him… "You say if I have the faith of a mustard seed, you will move a mountain. Well, I have the faith of a mountain, and I KNOW that you can do this. I have faith that you can do this. Just please let us pass…"

I never took my foot off of the gas and with that prayer, we got just a little bit of traction at first and then we slowly just drove out of there. We drove like that with the water over the hood of my pathfinder about a thousand yards. The water never came into the car. And the engine never stalled. A miracle of miracles. Praise the Lord!

Isaiah 43:2 When thou passest through the waters, I will be with thee; and through the rivers, they shall not overflow thee: when thou walkest through the fire, thou shalt not be burned; neither shall the flame kindle upon thee.

We got to my brother's house and of course, they had no idea what was going on. It was still dark outside, and they were sleeping. We had been frantically calling them and got them on the phone right before arriving. As soon as I got out of the car, I collapsed in my brother's arms.

We still didn't believe that the water could have made it into the house. Because like I said… It was a big hill. My brother and I went over there when the authorities said it was clear to go back to the house. There were police at the entrance to the neighborhood checking identification, because after a flood everybody has to pull out all of their belongings to dry and looters will come and steal everything. What a world.

Through the next few months there were many miracles that manifested His sweet love and care for us as we had to rebuild our house. I won't go into all of them, but I will say this. He used that experience not only to build my faith, but to plant many seeds with everyone I came in contact with after that. Even my insurance agent commented on my good mood for having lost so much. I told Him that Jesus saved my life that day and I could give a crap about the house. After hearing the story, he told me that there was no reason for me to be alive. I knew that, and that is why I keep telling everyone. He would tell me later that he shared that with his wife and everyone he knew and in his office. The Way…

Below are pictures. One is of the flood hours after, when my brother and I went back to assess the damage. The other is my pathfinder. The license plate unscrewed and bent in half with the force of the water. What a miracle… Thank you Jesus for sparing our lives!

Chapter 12

The Not so Great, Not so much a Mystery, Babylon

Many of you have heard about the tower of Babel (which literally means confusion). Mankind built a tower to try and be able to get to heaven. Of course, without God. Before that, the whole earth spoke one language which made things very easy. God had told them to go forth throughout the earth to multiply and populate it.

So, instead of obeying God, they came to Shinar (which is modern day Iraq) and decided to stop there and build a city and the tower to heaven. Their pride in thinking they knew better than God was their downfall. Sound familiar? Could this even have been the first asherah pole?

God saw what they were doing and confounded their language and scattered them. (Thanks a lot guys!)

Fast forward to Saul, who was our first man king. God had wanted not only to be our God but our King. Did we accept that? No, of course not!

1 Samuel 8:7 And the Lord said unto Samuel, Hearken unto the voice of the people in all that they say unto thee: for they have not rejected thee, but they have rejected me, that I should not reign over them.

And then God said fine, I won't be your king as you ask, but this is what you're going to get:

1 Samuel 8:11-19 And he said, This will be the manner of the king that shall reign over you: He will take your sons, and appoint them for himself, for his chariots, and to be his horsemen; and some shall run before his chariots. And he will appoint him captains over thousands, and captains over fifties; and will set them to ear his ground, and to reap his harvest, and to make his instruments of war, and instruments of his chariots. And he will take your daughters to be confectionaries, and to be cooks, and to be bakers. And he will take your fields, and your vineyards, and your oliveyards, even the best of them, and give them to his servants. And he will take the tenth of your seed, and of your vineyards, and give to his officers, and to his servants. And he will take your menservants, and your maidservants, and your goodliest young men, and your asses, and put them to his work. He will take the tenth of your sheep: and ye shall be his servants. And ye shall cry out in that day because of your king which ye shall have chosen you; and the Lord will not hear you in that day. Nevertheless the people refused to obey the voice of Samuel; and they said, Nay; but we will have a king over us;

After all of that, they still said Nah, we will take our chances. We are still suffering under everything that God described way back then today. Nothing new under the sun.

King Nebuchadnezzar, who was the king of Babylon, had a dream about what was to come of the kingdoms of the earth and the man kings that we asked God for...

Daniel 2:32-35 This image's head was of fine gold, his breast and his arms of silver, his belly and his thighs of brass, His legs of iron, his feet part of iron and part of clay. Thou sawest till that a stone was cut out without hands, which smote the image upon his feet that were of iron and clay, and brake them to pieces. Then was the iron, the clay, the brass, the silver, and the gold, broken to pieces together, and became like the chaff of the summer threshingfloors; and the wind carried them away, that no place was found for them: and the stone that smote the image became a great mountain, and filled the whole earth.

Daniel interpreted that dream for him by asking God what it meant, which is always a good practice. He told him that Nebuchadnezzar was the golden head and basically the rest were other kingdoms to come. I'm not going to go into who those are but that is an interesting study. Although, no one really knows for sure. Long story short, Christ our cornerstone is going to come back and smote them and setup His Kingdom and fill the whole earth with His Dominion.

Nebuchadnezzar also erected a man of gold that he demanded everyone to worship. Turns out that may be the same place of the tower of Babel at Shinar…

Daneil 3:1 Nebuchadnezzar the king made an image of gold, whose height was threescore cubits, and the breadth thereof six cubits: he set it up in the plain of Dura, in the province of Babylon.

Three score and six is 60 times 6. It is interesting that the numbers are around 6 don't you think? Even more interesting, I just googled this story and many of the translations have changed it to 90 times 9. The deception is growing worse by the day. And now, with artificial intelligence, they are literally re-writing everything. Keep your books and bibles folks to teach your children.

Anyway, Nebuchadnezzar had made a decree that everyone would worship this image including the Hebrew children that they had taken from Jerusalem. Shadrach, Meshach and Abednego. They were devout Jews and faithful to God so they refused and were tossed in the fiery furnace for it. When they looked in the furnace there were actually four figures in there and scripture says one looked to be the Son of God.

Not one hair was singed on those children, and I think this is a beautiful story to remember as we go into some very hard times. God's wings can protect His children from anything. He will walk through the fire with us.

Nebuchadnezzar had yet another dream, about a huge tree that the height thereof reached into heaven and in that tree, there was fruit and meat for all flesh.

Daniel 4:23 And whereas the king saw a watcher and an holy one coming down from heaven, and saying, Hew the tree down, and destroy it; yet leave the stump of the roots thereof in the earth, even with a band of iron and brass, in the tender grass of the field; and let it be wet with the dew of heaven, and let his portion be with the beasts of the field, till seven times pass over him;

You should already know who that tree is that gets cut down. The stump and the roots thereof are the fallen angels reserved in chains.

Daniel interpreted all of this about Nebuchadnezzar and his kingdom back then which came true. He roamed around outside for seven years after this dream without his kingdom. But as I keep repeating, everything usually has more than one meaning.

That dream was also for the end of Babylon in this world (Confusion and Un-Godliness) and all human kingdoms along with the prince of this world and the angels that have been chained up this whole time. That whole upside-down world they created will be cut down and finally pulled out by the roots and thrown into the fire.

Revelation talks about mystery Babylon herself riding on the beast. When is that happening? Before Jesus gets here, I can tell you that!

Revelation 17:3-5 So he carried me away in the spirit into the wilderness: and I saw a woman sit upon a scarlet coloured beast, full of names of blasphemy, having seven heads and ten horns. And the woman was arrayed in purple and scarlet colour, and decked with gold and precious stones and pearls, having a golden cup in her hand full of abominations and filthiness of her fornication: And upon her forehead was a name written, Mystery, Babylon The Great, The Mother Of Harlots And Abominations Of The Earth.

This "beast" is the upside-down of this world. This is the spirit of the devil and his angels that causes confusion. He makes us think that what is wrong is right. What is easy is hard. What is abominable is love. What is precious is fantasy. He is the author of confusion. He is the father of lies.

John 8:44 Ye are of your father the devil, and the lusts of your father ye will do. He was a murderer from the beginning, and abode not in the truth, because there is no truth in him. When he speaketh a lie, he speaketh of his own: for he is a liar, and the father of it.

This confusion and deception is in every part of our world. Government, Financial, Church, Education, everywhere. Should that upset us and worry us? NO! It was written and has to come to pass. We are living in Babylon, the upside-down, the state of ultimate confusion.

As for the interpretation of the beast, Revelation declares that too. People act like it is too hard to understand, but I think that is just another lie of the enemy. Why would he want us to know that he has no chance. He wants us to be afraid of him and doubt our King.

Revelation 17: 9 And here is the mind which hath wisdom. The seven heads are seven mountains, on which the woman sitteth.

There are seven continents in this world: Asia, Africa, North America, South America, Antarctica, Europe, and Australia (listed from largest to smallest in size) That great whore is all who are deceived in this world and follow after satan. They are whores because they forgot their first love (Jesus) and followed after him.

Revelation 17:10 And there are seven kings: five are fallen, and one is, and the other is not yet come; and when he cometh, he must continue a short space.

This goes with Nebuchadnezzar's dream of the man made of different metals all representing different kingdoms. Five have fallen and one is under the golden head of "Babylon".

The other who has not yet come and has a short space. Guess who that is? Satan at the 6th trump, the 6th vial and the 6th seal. The only thing we have to fear is fear itself. But fear is dispelled with knowledge. As long as you know what's coming, it's not scary. You know how the book ends! It's scary to choose to stay in darkness and ignorance because that is where you can lose your soul.

Revelation 17:11 And the beast that was, and is not, even he is the eighth, and is of the seven, and goeth into perdition.

This is also Satan... It is stated that he is released after Jesus comes with his saints to teach for a thousand years. This is the millennium. Anyone that doesn't get it after being with Christ for a thousand years probably deserves to go into perdition with the devil. We don't want them with us.

Revelation 20:2-3 And he laid hold on the dragon, that old serpent, which is the Devil, and Satan, and bound him a thousand years, And cast him into the bottomless pit, and shut him up, and set a seal upon him, that he should deceive the nations no more, till the thousand years should be fulfilled: and after that he must be loosed a little season.

Revelation 17:12-13 And the ten horns which thou sawest are ten kings, which have received no kingdom as yet; but receive power as kings one hour with the beast. These have one mind, and shall give their power and strength unto the beast.

These are ten kings that satan will put in power with him. We haven't seen this yet and you will know and recognize them because you will be praying for discernment, and the Holy Spirit will not let you be deceived if you ask him to show you and teach you.

Revelation 17:14 These shall make war with the Lamb, and the Lamb shall overcome them: for he is Lord of lords, and King of kings: and they that are with him are called, and chosen, and faithful.

Told you… you just gotta read the back of the book!

Revelation 17:15 And he saith unto me, The waters which thou sawest, where the whore sitteth, are peoples, and multitudes, and nations, and tongues.

They deceive the whole world with their upside-down government, financial schemes, education and religions.

Revelation 17:16-18 And the ten horns which thou sawest upon the beast, these shall hate the whore, and shall make her desolate and naked, and shall eat her flesh, and burn her with fire. For God hath put in their hearts to fulfil his will, and to agree, and give their kingdom unto the beast, until the words of God shall be fulfilled. And the woman which thou sawest is that great city, which reigneth over the kings of the earth.

Again, those ten horns are ten kings and their government that satan brings in with him. The ultimate of deception. But notice, it says God has put in their hearts to fulfill His will. He is always in control. Is it His will that all of this destruction happen? No, but I think it has to happen to fulfill the Word of God. It has to happen to destroy satan's children and the fallen angels. And, ultimately, it has to happen to save all of God's children. Otherwise, we have no hope.

Old mystery Babylon herself… The confusion that we chose from the beginning in the Garden to the end. And all those flesh kings we asked for in between. We chose it. If we had just trusted the One who created and love us.

Chapter 13

Godincidences

I have had a lot of close calls in my life. Big and small, where I know in my heart that God has intervened. In everyday life, these things happen all the time. Missing an accident on the highway because you lost your keys. A phone call made you late, so you were there for an emergency at your house. There are a thousand different scenarios. Is that completely random or is there something divine protecting you?

I've always loved this story because it has justified my love of gambling that started on this trip…

My parents LOVED to gamble. So, it was natural for them to take me to Vegas on my 21st birthday.

My mom's first husband was in the Air Force and had died in a test flight. Because of this, she was pretty nervous on airplanes. My dad was a pilot himself and loved to fly and I shared that love as well. We decided to buy tickets on an airplane tour over the Grand Canyon while in Vegas. My Mom wanted no part of this… so it was just my dad and me.

The day before we were supposed to go on the tour, I convinced my dad to take a craps class with me. I'd seen that game in the casino but neither of my parents had played and it looked like fun to me. The casino had a free class where you could play with play money and not lose anything to learn. I fell in love with it! My Dad liked it but not as much as I did. So, he went back to playing slots and I went on my first craps adventure.

I was so successful that I didn't get home until the wee hours of the morning. My parents were not so happy with me that it was so late, but when they saw all the chips they just laughed and told me to go to bed.

I woke up and my parents had left a note that they were at breakfast. So, I got ready and went downstairs… I had completely forgotten about the flight we booked over the Grand Canyon. My Dad was teasing me that he hoped it was worth it to miss my only chance to see it. We laughed and finished breakfast and went back to the casino and didn't think twice about it.

Later that afternoon we got back to the hotel room to several desperate messages from my family. Apparently, the exact plane that we had booked, and didn't show up for, had crashed and killed everyone on it. We were just stunned…

There wasn't anything as dramatic as a voice telling us not to get on that plane. But, I believe with all my heart that God put me in circumstances to avoid that accident. Why am I saved and not those people? I wish I knew the answer to that question… maybe it is to write this book to hopefully convince at least one of God's existence. I wasn't done yet. And, neither are you… If you are still breathing, He has a purpose for your life.

Was it a coincidence that I happened to stay out gambling and slept late? I don't think so… It was a Godincidence.

I was lucky enough to live overseas with one of my best friends in my twenties. I had made some money and was not married and didn't have any kids, so I thought it was the time to do it if I was ever going to have that chance. It was a decision that changed my life, and I have cherished all of those memories.

Travel expands your universe and life. It gives you greater understanding of others and evidence of how vast and how amazing God's creation truly is.

We had rented a car and were touring in Spain. Our plan was to make it all the way down to the Rock of Gibraltar and then take the boat over into Morocco. We were going to spend a few days shopping and eating there and then take a flight to Istanbul. We had a friend from there and his family could help us if we got in trouble.

We made it to Sevilla (which was amazing)! While there, we heard that the president of Morocco had fallen over dead in New York with a heart attack. We had some friends in Brussels that were Moroccan, so we called them to ask if it was still safe to go.

They told us it was completely safe. However, they were fasting because they were mourning. So, no restaurants and all the shops were closed. Hmmm… I think we can come up with a better plan. We thought ok, we will just get back to Madrid and try to go straight to Istanbul from there.

We were literally sitting in the Madrid airport trying to change our tickets, when my friend received an urgent call from her work. She was in network management, and they needed her to come back immediately to fix some issues that had come up. So, we changed our ticket to go back to Brussels and just thought we would regroup from there.

We made it home that night and when we woke up Istanbul was all over the news. There had been a massive earthquake there that killed thousands of people.

Was it a coincidence that her work diverted us? I don't think so… It was a Godincidence.

These are two drastic examples, but as I said, I think these things happen every day. Ask God to show you, how He has protected you and guided you. Ask Him to do so and reveal it to you. You will be surprised to see how He has and does have His hand on you.

Chapter 14

The Church

Jeremiah 23:1-2 Woe be unto the pastors that destroy and scatter the sheep of my pasture! saith the Lord. Therefore thus saith the Lord God of Israel against the pastors that feed my people; Ye have scattered my flock, and driven them away, and have not visited them: behold, I will visit upon you the evil of your doings, saith the Lord.

Truth is, most all of us believe in a higher power. That power exists and is God. The geographical location where we grew up normally dictates how we worship for the most part. That worship is the foundation of our being and as discussed, the only thing that fills the hole in our hearts. It is the reason for our existence.

However, the difference in worship or denominations/divisions do exactly that. They divide, when we are all supposed to be ONE body under Christ.

1 Corinthians 12:12-13 For as the body is one, and hath many members, and all the members of that one body, being many, are one body: so also is Christ. For by one Spirit are we all baptized into one body, whether we be Jews or Gentiles, whether we be bond or free; and have been all made to drink into one Spirit.

The devil knows about that hole in your heart also and wants you to worship him… and he loves to twist evil things and make them sound sooooooo religious. Before you know it, you are worshipping him without even knowing it. God warned us of this long ago.

2 Peter 2:1-3 But there were false prophets also among the people, even as there shall be false teachers among you, who privily shall bring in damnable heresies, even denying the Lord that bought them, and bring upon themselves swift destruction. And many shall follow their pernicious ways; by reason of whom the way of truth shall be evil spoken of. And through covetousness shall they with feigned words make merchandise of you: whose judgment now of a long time lingereth not, and their damnation slumbereth not.

If you are not reading your bible, you are endangering yourself to be deceived by the devil and even your preachers. I know that is a strong statement but it's true. He has foretold us all things and you should be in the Word to understand them.

Luke 21:22-23 For false Christs and false prophets shall rise, and shall shew signs and wonders, to seduce, if it were possible, even the elect. But take ye heed: behold, I have foretold you all things.

How do you know if your preachers are false? Do they actually read from the bible and teach? Or do they just put up a few verses and then tell stories? That's a pretty good indication and sadly, the churches that actually teach the Word are hard to come by these days. It's no wonder that church attendance around the world is down. They aren't feeding God's children the Bread of Life.

2 Timothy 4:3-4 For the time will come when they will not endure sound doctrine; but after their own lusts shall they heap to themselves teachers, having itching ears; And they shall turn away their ears from the truth, and shall be turned unto fables.

Jesus even quoted Isaiah on this topic, knowing that man would listen to each other and not the Word of God. Teaching doctrines of men likely inspired by the evil one himself.

Matthew 15:7-9 Ye hypocrites, well did Esaias prophesy of you, saying, This people draweth nigh unto me with their mouth, and honoureth me with their lips; but their heart is far from me. But in vain they do worship me, teaching for doctrines the commandments of men.

One of the very first things Jesus did when He came into Jerusalem was to clean up the church!

Matthew 21:12-13 And Jesus went into the temple of God, and cast out all them that sold and bought in the temple, and overthrew the tables of the moneychangers, and the seats of them that sold doves, And said unto them, It is written, My house shall be called the house of prayer; but ye have made it a den of thieves.

People from the tribes of Israel are all over this world. Assyria captured the northern ten tribes in 720 BC and God then scattered them, they are still "lost". Remember there are twelve tribes. Judah and Benjamin are primarily what is considered "Israel" in Israel. The rest… God scattered them long ago and most have no idea who they are.

1 Kings 14:15 For the Lord shall smite Israel, as a reed is shaken in the water, and he shall root up Israel out of this good land, which he gave to their fathers, and shall scatter them beyond the river, because they have made their groves, provoking the Lord to anger.

You might remember the "groves" from the discussion on the asherah poles and baal worship.

Prior to bringing Jacob (all twelve tribes) back together in the end times, the Lord will pour out His Spirit upon them and there will be healing in his wings.

Malachi 4:2 But unto you that fear my name shall the Sun of righteousness arise with healing in his wings; and ye shall go forth, and grow up as calves of the stall.

Ezekiel talked about the dry bones coming to life. How did they come back to life? God told Ezekiel to prophecy to them. Teach them the Word of God. That is symbolic of our spirits in this world. We need to be taught and then He will fill us with that Ruach, the very breath of life given by God.

Ezekiel 37:1-5 The hand of the Lord was upon me, and carried me out in the spirit of the Lord, and set me down in the midst of the valley which was full of bones, And caused me to pass by them round about: and, behold, there were very many in the open valley; and, lo, they were very dry. And he said unto me, Son of man, can these bones live? And I answered, O Lord God, thou knowest. Again he said unto me, Prophesy upon these bones, and say unto them, O ye dry bones, hear the word of the Lord. Thus saith the Lord God unto these bones; Behold, I will cause breath to enter into you, and ye shall live:

He will join Israel (ten northern tribes) and Judah back together again and place them in His Kingdom as it was promised long ago in Ezekiel.

Ezekiel 37:19-28 Say unto them, Thus saith the Lord God; Behold, I will take the stick of Joseph, which is in the hand of Ephraim, and the tribes of Israel his fellows, and will put them with him, even with the stick of Judah, and make them one stick, and they shall be one in mine hand. And the sticks whereon thou writest shall be in thine hand before their eyes. And say unto them, Thus saith the Lord God; Behold, I will take the children of Israel from among the heathen, whither they be gone, and will gather them on every side, and bring them into their own land: And I will make them one nation in the land upon the mountains of Israel; and one king shall be king to them all: and they shall be no more two nations, neither shall they be divided into two kingdoms any more at all. Neither shall they defile themselves any more with their idols, nor with their detestable things, nor with any of their transgressions: but I will save them out of all their dwellingplaces, wherein they have sinned, and will cleanse them: so shall they be my people, and I will be their God. And David my servant shall be king over them; and they all shall have one shepherd: they shall also walk in my judgments, and observe my statutes, and do them. And they shall dwell in the land that I have given unto Jacob my servant, wherein your fathers have dwelt; and they shall dwell therein, even they, and their children, and their children's children for ever: and my servant David shall be their prince for ever. Moreover I will make a covenant of peace with them; it shall be an everlasting covenant with them: and I will place them, and multiply them, and will set my sanctuary in the midst of them for evermore. My tabernacle also shall be with them: yea, I will be their God, and they shall be my people. And the heathen shall know that I the Lord do sanctify Israel, when my sanctuary shall be in the midst of them for evermore.

He is faithful to his promises and will draw you to Himself in these end times. There is nothing to be afraid of… I bet many of you are hearing this for the first time. And that is ok. God has you reading this book for a reason. To begin to have the scales fall from your eyes.

Again, you need to be in the Word yourself to avoid confusion (Babylon). God has foretold you all things and there eventually comes a punishment for not listening to your Father. There is a great deception coming from satan and you need to be prepared.

Isaiah 47:13 Thou art wearied in the multitude of thy counsels. Let now the astrologers, the stargazers, the monthly prognosticators, stand up, and save thee from these things that shall come upon thee.

I think all of the little twists in all of the religions are ultimately designed by the devil. I believe he uses that to confuse us and distract us from the simplicity of the Word of God, which is Christ Jesus. He even tried to tempt Jesus with scripture. The Word of God walking among us. That is how brazen he is!

Matthew 4:5-7 Then the devil taketh him up into the holy city, and setteth him on a pinnacle of the temple, And saith unto him, If thou be the Son of God, cast thyself down: for it is written, He shall give his angels charge concerning thee: and in their hands they shall bear thee up, lest at any time thou dash thy foot against a stone. Jesus said unto him, It is written again, Thou shalt not tempt the Lord thy God.

I know this sounds crazy… but I've seen, if not the devil, a demon in a church service sitting about five rows in front of me. I remember looking at him and thinking that he was really good looking! Of course he was… the bible talks about how beautiful God made him.

He was sitting at the edge of the row against the wall and was wearing a three-piece suit and tie. He was dressed extremely well, but more for the 1800s than now and it should have registered with me that no one dresses like that. He also had several rings on and looked extremely wealthy.

Once the music started and everyone stood up, I realized how tall he was. Like ten feet tall! I just kept staring at him. The preacher encouraged us to pray individually for part of the song and there was another man in his row. He walked over to him and put his arm around him. He proceeded to sort of hug him/pat him, but it wasn't sincere. Hard to explain but it was fake, and the man didn't even know it was happening. He didn't acknowledge him at all even though he was touching him. Then he just walked back to his seat against the wall and sat down.

By then I started to realize that this is a vision. I started praying asking God if He wanted me to confront him or what I needed to do here. After the service, I started walking towards him and here comes a friend of mine shouting my name all the way from the front of the church. Everyone in that room looked at me, except him. He held his eyes forward and never stood up. He also didn't even glance in my direction despite the spectacle that my friend made.

The armor of God is a real thing and if you have it, the evil ones cannot even look in your direction. Much less harm you. Do not be afraid of them.

Ephesians 6:11-17 Put on the whole armour of God, that ye may be able to stand against the wiles of the devil. For we wrestle not against flesh and blood, but against principalities, against powers, against the rulers of the darkness of this world, against spiritual wickedness in high places. Wherefore take unto you the whole armour of God, that ye may be able to withstand in the evil day, and having done all, to stand. Stand therefore, having your loins girt about with truth, and having on the breastplate of righteousness; And your feet shod with the preparation of the gospel of peace; Above all, taking the shield of faith, wherewith ye shall be able to quench all the fiery darts of the wicked. And take the helmet of salvation, and the sword of the Spirit, which is the word of God:

The bible instructs us to study, commune and take care of each other. However, religion breeds separation and judgement. The word denomination literally means division. We are supposed to be learning together and encouraging each other. Not judging other "divisions".

There is nothing in the bible that says that you have to be a good Baptist or good Catholic or Jew or Jehovah's Witness to get into heaven. It's faith in Christ as He is the WAY and absorbing His Word which is literally and figuratively Him. There is healing in His Word, and you are cheating yourself if you aren't feeding your soul with it.

As a matter of fact, that is why God sent His Son to die for us. He had given us the law through Moses, because He saw the evil that was being done. We broke all of those laws with the enchantments and sin that the fallen angels had taught us and continue to tempt us with.

So, when he saw that there was no way for us, of our own accord, to live without sin. He sent His own son as the scapegoat to cover our sins so that we could be with Him. The ultimate sacrifice for one and all time.

To heal us from our sin and bring us back to God. Because He knew that we could never live under the law and not break it. Sin had already infiltrated this world by satan and his angels.

Romans 8:1-3 There is therefore now no condemnation to them which are in Christ Jesus, who walk not after the flesh, but after the Spirit. For the law of the Spirit of life in Christ Jesus hath made me free from the law of sin and death. For what the law could not do, in that it was weak through the flesh, God sending his own Son in the likeness of sinful flesh, and for sin, condemned sin in the flesh:

Most churches are performance based. You are respected for how "good" you are or at least appear to be. They say different, but much of the preaching is around how you should act as a Christian. And is most often based on traditions of men, instead of learning the word of God and allowing the Spirit to lead your life.

Hear me... you could never be good enough or pious enough to be in God's courts without Jesus. He is the light, and The Way and the only way for you to become Holy and set apart to Him. He sent Jesus to save us NOT condemn us.

John 3:16-18 For God so loved the world, that he gave his only begotten Son, that whosoever believeth in him should not perish, but have everlasting life. For God sent not his Son into the world to condemn the world; but that the world through him might be saved. He that believeth on him is not condemned: but he that believeth not is condemned already, because he hath not believed in the name of the only begotten Son of God.

Chapter 15

The Anti-Christ

I am not going to pretend that I know everything about what is coming. No one does. But, I do know that it is coming because God's word says it's coming and I think you can probably feel it. I know there is no rapture by Christ because that is not in God's word. I know that the anti-christ, the devil will come before Jesus pretending to be Him to deceive the world. I believe likely as christ coming to rapture his "church" and those who have not studied (even many good Christians) will follow him. And then when the real Christ comes, they will pray for the mountains to fall on them out of embarrassment and sadness at being deceived. That is all scriptural.

What will it be like when he steps onto the scene?

2 Timothy 3:3-5 For men shall be lovers of their own selves, covetous, boasters, proud, blasphemers, disobedient to parents, unthankful, unholy, Without natural affection, trucebreakers, false accusers, incontinent, fierce, despisers of those that are good, Traitors, heady, highminded, lovers of pleasures more than lovers of God; Having a form of godliness, but denying the power thereof: from such turn away.

I'd say that pretty much sums up what we see in our world today.

No man knoweth the time or place of Jesus' return.

Matthew 24:36 But of that day and hour knoweth no man, no, not the angels of heaven, but my Father only.

And, anyone that tells you different is a liar and mark them as a false prophet. Jesus warned us of this also…

Matthew 24:11 And many false prophets shall rise, and shall deceive many.

How do I know there is no rapture? Because it is not in the bible and the Holy Spirit has led me to know that it is evil.

I recently went on a cruise where the rapture theory was taught. I had been told about this teacher by a co-worker of mine and felt the Holy Spirit's leading to follow him. He is a really good teacher, and I got a lot out of his newsletters and teachings.

One of the emails I received was about this cruise covering Revelation and Daniel. I got that burning in my chest again that He does when He wants me to do something. So this time, I didn't delay and booked it. Over the next few months, I realized that he taught the rapture theory. I thought well, maybe I'm wrong and God wants to show me.

The very first day I was in the group for the first meet and greet with him. (There were several throughout the cruise.) I'm thinking… what in the world am I going to say to this guy. I've only been following him for a few months, and he is like the Elvis of preachers to his followers that have all been following him for years.

As I'm standing in line, the thought occurs to me. I'll show him the picture I have of Jesus that I took on the Mount of Olives. (the one on the cover of this book) Surely, he will be amazed at that and excited to see a picture of his Savior! Who wouldn't be?

I'll tell you who… this guy!

I've never seen a demon recoil, but that is the closest description I can think of to his reaction. Once he saw it, he wouldn't look at it or me anymore. He was cutting me off and saying, "yeah, an image, yeah, I saw it an image". And, trying to get me out of there as quickly as possible. Again, they can't even look at you if you have Jesus inside you.

Hardly the reaction that you would think from a Christian preacher. I'm telling you… There is evil everywhere these days and you need to pray for discernment. And the best protection you have is to read your bibles and learn from the Holy Spirit. Do not take it from me or anyone else.

Here is the main verse that the rapture theory comes from:

1 Thessalonians 4:17 Then we which are alive and remain shall be caught up together with them in the clouds, to meet the Lord in the air: and so shall we ever be with the Lord.

Now here is that verse with the verses around it for context:

1 Thessalonians 4:13-18 But I would not have you to be ignorant, brethren, concerning them which are asleep, that ye sorrow not, even as others which have no hope. For if we believe that Jesus died and rose again, even so them also which sleep in Jesus will God bring with him. For this we say unto you by the word of the Lord, that we which are alive and remain unto the coming of the Lord shall not prevent them which are asleep. For the Lord himself shall descend from heaven with a shout, with the voice of the archangel, and with the trump of God: and the dead in Christ shall rise first: Then we which are alive and remain shall be caught up together with them in the clouds, to meet the Lord in the air: and so shall we ever be with the Lord. Wherefore comfort one another with these words.

The subject is the dead who are already with Christ. That word "prevent" them, is precede in Greek and of course we wouldn't precede them because they are dead and already risen into His presence. The "air" is God's spirit. Jesus is coming here to setup His Kingdom for ever and ever. Reference the Lord's prayer in Chapter 8 - Jesus. Everything will be put back as it was. There will be no heaven and earth. It will all be here and one and perfect. So, the air, the clouds, the earth and us… everything will be in God's Ruach which is a beautiful Hebrew word meaning the breath of God, Spirit, Wind, Air and Life.

Even the Thessalonians were confused by these verses. So, Paul wrote 2 Thessalonians, a second letter to explain it further to them.

2 Thessalonians 2:3-4 Let no man deceive you by any means: for that day shall not come, except there come a falling away first, and that man of sin be revealed, the son of perdition; Who opposeth and exalteth himself above all that is called God, or that is worshipped; so that he as God sitteth in the temple of God, shewing himself that he is God.

The actual rapture theory itself came from a man named John Nelson Darby in the 1800s. It is believed that he got his revelation for this theory from Margaret MacDonald who was part of a charismatic group in Scotland. After her healing, she began speaking in tongues. You can go online and read the transcript of what she said.

There are many that believed those utterances by MacDonald were demonic. I read it and it really doesn't sound to me even what the rapture theory now represents. But I agree, that what was taken from those utterances and put forth in the church is demonic. It is taught as gospel when it is a tradition of man. Which…will…always…get…us… in…trouble!!!

We can argue about scripture and whether or not what I'm saying is true. I simply ask you to pray for discernment and the leading of the Holy Spirit and read it for yourself. All of it in context, not just one verse.

But hear me loud and clear on this…If you are not in the Ruach/Spirit when "christ" tells you to get on the boat for the rapture. Do NOT GO!! That is one way to KNOW that he is not christ.

Matthew 24:23-26 Then if any man shall say unto you, Lo, here is Christ, or there; believe it not. For there shall arise false Christs, and false prophets, and shall shew great signs and wonders; insomuch that, if it were possible, they shall deceive the very elect. Behold, I have told you before. Wherefore if they shall say unto you, Behold, he is in the desert; go not forth: behold, he is in the secret chambers; believe it not.

One of the most gross cover ups in the newer bible translations comes from Ezekiel. Here is what it says from the King James version which is the one I read, and it was already translated improperly:

Ezekiel 13:16-21 To wit, the prophets of Israel which prophesy concerning Jerusalem, and which see visions of peace for her, and there is no peace, saith the Lord God. Likewise, thou son of man, set thy face against the daughters of thy people, which prophesy out of their own heart; and prophesy thou against them, And say, Thus saith the Lord God; Woe to the women that sew pillows to all armholes, and make kerchiefs upon the head of every stature to hunt souls! Will ye hunt the souls of my people, and will ye save the souls alive that come unto you? And will ye pollute me among my people for handfuls of barley and for pieces of bread, to slay the souls that should not die, and to save the souls alive that should not live, by your lying to my people that hear your lies? Wherefore thus saith the Lord God; Behold, I am against your pillows, wherewith ye there hunt the souls to make them fly, and I will tear them from your arms, and will let the souls go, even the souls that ye hunt to make them fly. Your kerchiefs also will I tear, and deliver my people out of your hand, and they shall be no more in your hand to be hunted; and ye shall know that I am the Lord.

What in the heck is he talking about? It sounds crazy because the translations have been messed up. I fully believe satan has had his hand in the translations of the bible. Of course he has! Those pillows and armholes originally described coverings to cover my outstretched saving hands. Concealing the salvation available to them. Makes sense that satan would want to cover that up. And how is he teaching them to save themselves now? To fly away to save their souls. That is exactly how he hunts them!

If Revelation intimidates you to read, you can teach practically the entire book of Revelation from Matthew 24. All of the gospels proclaim His coming. Mark 13, Luke 21 and John 14. Those are four different witnesses to what Jesus proclaimed himself to his disciples while He was with us. To lovingly prepare us for His return and the coming of the evil one before Him.

That whole mark of the beast thing in the movies about 666 is true. I don't know if that is a physical mark, but it comes from Revelation. The ant-christ comes at the 6th trump, the 6th seal and the 6th vile. Jesus comes at the 7th trump, the 7th seal and the 7th vile. It is not hard to figure out who comes first. But our churches don't teach this. We are sorely unprepared for what is coming.

Revelation 13:18 Here is wisdom. Let him that hath understanding count the number of the beast: for it is the number of a man; and his number is Six hundred threescore and six.

Think about it this way as well... God has literally gone through creating the earth, then destroying it completely, creating it again, then flooding it, and then repopulating and then sending his own Son to die so that we can be saved. Do you think he is going to pull all of his remnant out of here and just leave the rest of his children to the devil without any help?

That is not God's nature and not how He has shown Himself to be to us. He has literally chased us to the ends of the earth! Twice! He is not going to leave us now.

But that sure does sound like a lie that somebody else would tell you!

I know I'm repeating myself, but it is important, and your soul depends on it. I'm telling you that you need to open your bibles and let the Holy Spirit teach your spirit for yourself. He will call things to your remembrance that you already know in your spirit, and it is a beautiful daily revelation from the lover of your soul.

Chapter 16

The Dragon

God drew me to write this book to a place called Noto, Sicily. I had only been to Sicily for a few hours on that cruise I mentioned. And I loved it!

Long story short, I bought two paintings on my cruise. One that was similar to the square here in Noto and the other looked like the actual place where I would stay the whole time while writing. I didn't know that at the time that I was purchasing those paintings in Rome and Greece respectively.

As I was boarding the plane home from the cruise, I got that burning again when I saw the main square of Noto on Facebook that not so randomly came up on my feed. I knew that was where I had to go next. I'm learning to just do it as they say… Similarly, I found the B&B that God had directed me to that looked like the other painting and left right after the holidays.

I got to Noto on New Year's Day evening with a dead phone and no taxis at the bus station. I looked to the right and there was Hotel Flora. My mother's name was Flora… sweet little God winks. I walked in and they had a plate for the change that said Hotel Flora with a ladybug, which has been my little sign from Him of protection and love. Everything is going to be ok! I was able to get a hold of the B&B and they came to get me.

The next day I had to walk into the town for a charger, which is a whole book on its own featuring a road that I should not have been walking on, through hills with zero visibility cutbacks, going the wrong way, and more nice people helping me. Talk about walking by faith. I realized later the adapter that I had brought didn't fit my notebook to write this book so a divine solution to a problem that I didn't even know that I had. Always a step ahead of us thank God!

A few days later, I went back into town to actually see some of the sites and look at the Christmas lights before they took them down. The sky started doing a crazy thing again. So as I do, I took pictures. Turns out, there was the dragon in the sky this time.

I did take note at how small and insignificant the image was in the sky compared to the photo of Jesus that I took. You can see the original image and then the upside down blown-up focused images.

I looked up the astronomy report for that day on astronomy.com and here is what it said:

Earth reached perihelion this morning when our planet's not-quite circular orbit brings us to our closest point to the Sun for the year. Hmmm…

The moon passes .7 degrees north of 1st magnitude Saturn (satan's representative planet). The two are 3 degrees apart with the Moon to saturn's upper left in the sky and bright Venus (Jesus' representative planet) to the lower right.

I'm not an astrologer but it sounds like something is going on up there... and it sure looks like it from here.

Revelation 12:9-12 And the great dragon was cast out, that old serpent, called the Devil, and Satan, which deceiveth the whole world: he was cast out into the earth, and his angels were cast out with him. And I heard a loud voice saying in heaven, Now is come salvation, and strength, and the kingdom of our God, and the power of his Christ: for the accuser of our brethren is cast down, which accused them before our God day and night. And they overcame him by the blood of the Lamb, and by the word of their testimony; and they loved not their lives unto the death. Therefore rejoice, ye heavens, and ye that dwell in them. Woe to the inhabiters of the earth and of the sea! for the devil is come down unto you, having great wrath, because he knoweth that he hath but a short time.

Luke 10:18 And he said unto them, I beheld Satan as lightning fall from heaven.

I had a dream about Machpelah which is the cave where Abraham, Sara, Isaac, Rebekah, Jacob and Leah are buried. There is lots of speculation as well that this is where the entrance to the garden of Eden was. I went there when I was in Israel, but did not really have any spiritual stirrings about that place at all. It was strange that the tomb representations of Abraham and Sara were split with one half being a Mosque and the other side being a Synagogue. You had to go out and around through a gate (guarded with machine guns) in between Israel and Palestinian held territories to view both sides.

I started doing some research online and I had forgotten that Eden is also supposed to be sort of the door between Heaven and Earth. Which got me thinking about this sighting of the dragon and why in the world God brought me here. It makes sense if Eden is the door that he would be kicked out there.

Sicily is one of the most beautiful places on earth I believe. It is full of caves also, so I started researching those but didn't really feel anything.

In the coming days and weeks, I had several people tell me that I needed to go to Malta. I had done one pass of this book and felt the Holy Spirit leading me there.

Malta is in the book of Acts, it was where Paul was shipwrecked on the way to Rome. He was bitten by a poisonous serpent there that came out of the fire. The people were amazed because he just shook it off back into the fire and continued teaching. They marveled that he did not die nor seem at all injured.

Side note that I learned while in Malta, that there have not been any poisonous snakes on that island ever since.

Anyway, chasing the source of this dragon, it seemed that the island with the serpent coming out of the fire was a good place to go. I was convinced that all of the mysteries of the Bible and religion that we had all been wondering about were going to be given to me there. Zippo…

I came back to Noto feeling defeated and that I had somehow let God down and missed it. He reminded me though of "The Way"… I had a terrible trip there through severe storms that included an extremely rough three-hour tour on the ferry boat. Getting the full Paul experience prior to the shipwreck!

But, through that experience and some others that I considered frustrating at the time, were beautiful connections and powerful seeds planted. I always think I know the purpose of things and I am almost always wrong. It's usually much more simple than my stupid flesh brain makes it and it's usually not about me. The last seed planted there in Malta was with a precious girl named Luz. "The light" in Spanish. I have no doubt she will be and I hope you read this, dear sweet special girl…

There was one place that I didn't go to on one of those hop on and off buses that I felt like I should have. It was a cave that I had not heard of but was by that point in the day done. I went back the next day and of course it was closed.

I looked up Ghar Dalam when I got back to Noto. Low and behold it is famous for its bees that live in the ground there. This sounds crazy, but I had a bee stuck in my wall in my house by its stinger upside down. I had been praying about it for God to reveal the meaning. Could this be a clue?

That cave housed Malta's earliest inhabitants dating back 7,000 years. (About the time of this earth age creation according to the bible) The name Malta itself even comes from the Greeks calling it Melite which is the land of honey. See what I mean by little breadcrumbs…

Another strange "bee" clue was that that the city of Avola, near where I am staying, is actually laid out like a beehive in a hexagon shape. 6 sides, 6 points… Also, very unusual.

Going back to the picture of the dragon. That is the right direction to where Malta lies. In addition to possibly Eden (which I am now thinking is Sicily), I believe Malta could also be Tyre or Tarshish. That city was known for being the center of trade and satan was the king of it. Malta is smack dab in the middle of the Mediterranean and all of the islands are full of natural harbors. Making it a natural center for trade. I found out now, it actually is a center for the drug trade in addition to all sorts of good coming from Africa, Europe, Greece and the Middle East.

Isaiah 23:14-18 Howl, ye ships of Tarshish: for your strength is laid waste. And it shall come to pass in that day, that Tyre shall be forgotten seventy years, according to the days of one king: after the end of seventy years shall Tyre sing as an harlot. And it shall come to pass after the end of seventy years, that the Lord will visit Tyre, and she shall turn to her hire, and shall commit fornication with all the kingdoms of the world upon the face of the earth. And her merchandise and her hire shall be holiness to the Lord: it shall not be treasured nor laid up; for her merchandise shall be for them that dwell before the Lord, to eat sufficiently, and for durable clothing.

Seventy years. Reminds me of the seven times from Daniel that the fallen angels are chained up. I don't know the starting point and no one else does either which is why only the Father knows the day and time. But I am seeing these things.

It's also not lost on me that I am on the island with Mount Etna. I just went to Santorini which is having multiple earthquakes a day. They are evacuating that island for fear of an eruption. Could it be that those fallen angels are chained up in our volcanoes? Like I said, God is very natural. It says they are chained up in the belly of the earth, and everything I've read about the fire and darkness that they would be in… Well, it makes sense.

Again, I think this could be those visions of the people/ants in the darkness crawling over each other trying to get out. He led me to this one about that vision with Jesus interpreting it for you. He has told us all things.

John 10:1-18 Verily, verily, I say unto you, He that entereth not by the door into the sheepfold, but climbeth up some other way, the same is a thief and a robber. But he that entereth in by the door is the shepherd of the sheep. To him the porter openeth; and the sheep hear his voice: and he calleth his own sheep by name, and leadeth them out. And when he putteth forth his own sheep, he goeth before them, and the sheep follow him: for they know his voice. And a stranger will they not follow, but will flee from him: for they know not the voice of strangers. This parable spake Jesus unto them: but they understood not what things they were which he spake unto them. Then said Jesus unto them again, Verily, verily, I say unto you, I am the door of the sheep. All that ever came before me are thieves and robbers: but the sheep did not hear them. I am the door: by me if any man enter in, he shall be saved, and shall go in and out, and find pasture. The thief cometh not, but for to steal, and to kill, and to destroy: I am come that they might have life, and that they might have it more abundantly. I am the good shepherd: the good shepherd giveth his life for the sheep. But he that is an hireling, and not the shepherd, whose own the sheep are not, seeth the wolf coming, and leaveth the sheep, and fleeth: and the wolf catcheth them, and scattereth the sheep. The hireling fleeth, because he is an hireling, and careth not for the sheep. I am the good shepherd, and know my sheep, and am known of mine. As the Father knoweth me, even so know I the Father: and I lay down my life for the sheep. And other sheep I have, which are not of this fold: them also I must bring, and they shall hear my voice; and there shall be one fold, and one shepherd. Therefore doth my Father love me, because I lay down my life, that I might take it again. No man taketh it from me, but I lay it down of myself. I have power to lay it down, and I have power to take it again. This commandment have I received of my Father.

The anti-christ will be supernatural and able to perform miracles. How do you think he is going to deceive most of the world?

Revelation 13: 11 And I beheld another beast coming up out of the earth; and he had two horns like a lamb, and he spake as a dragon.

Revelation 13:13 And he doeth great wonders, so that he maketh fire come down from heaven on the earth in the sight of men,

If you are not prepared, you will be taken in by this fake christ. Just get set that he is coming first and will perform miracles. There are a couple of things that he can't do… He can't read your mind, and he can't raise you into a spiritual body. I think most other things are on the table though so beware. He is a master illusionist.

Both sightings of Jesus and the dragon in the clouds were followed by major storms. With thousands of lightning strikes in them. Again, I don't fully understand what is going on there. But, baal was a canaanite god that was evil and associated with the devil, likely was the devil. He was also known as the storm God. The lightning bolt was even the symbol for him. It says satan can make lightning come down from heaven and the bible says thunder is the voice of God. So, I think these storms are actually battles taking place in heaven.

One of the storms in Noto after the dragon sighting even produced a tornado just down the street from us… God's protection. In going back over my notes, I realized that strangely I started a fast that same day. I had felt God pulling me to do that.

I believe fasting is a way to push down your flesh so your spiritual eyes can be opened. You will be surprised by the clarity that it brings. (Take note: You do have to build up to fast… if you are going to try it, research and start small and then continue to do it every several months when you feel God's leading)

As per usual though, there was more than one reason. I believe it had to do with warding off not only the physical attack of that tornado, but dealing with the visions that I am now going to tell you about. These are not meant to scare you but to prepare you and teach you how to deal with our enemy when he comes to you. There is nothing to fear because God has already defeated him.

Jesus disciples could cast out demons, but there were some that they couldn't cast out. And, when they asked Him why?

Mark 9:29 And he said unto them, This kind can come forth by nothing, but by prayer and fasting.

Like I said, I've had visions before. This was different. I'm not going to lie, it was scary. I was not asleep, as a matter of fact I had just turned the lights off to go to bed. So, I was not dreaming.

Night 1 of visions:

The ceiling started to change colors to greenish red and started swirling. Then, I saw things out of the corner of my eye. It looked like a cave wall with holes in it and scary things in them. I never looked at it directly. Because it scared the crap out of me!

So, as I've told you to do, I cast it away from me in Jesus' name. That seemed to work after a couple of minutes and started to fade away.

Then, there appeared an ancient presence on the ceiling. It looked like a monster with rigid skin but regal at the same time. Staring at me and just sort of hovering and sort of swirling itself. I don't know how to really describe it other than that. Terrifying, that's another way.

I was casting him out and it wasn't working. God then put in my mind a song. So, I started singing How Great Thou Art and it was making me cry. It didn't like that at all and started recoiling. So, I kept worshipping and praying and talking about how much I love God, and it swirled away slowly.

A pink-looking cloud filled the room and then came over me like a weighted blanket. It felt soothing and safe. It was also swirling and enveloped my face, but I could still breathe. I just laid there for a bit thanking God over and over again and telling him that I love Him.

Then, that started to dissipate, and the ceiling was reddish again with what looked like clouds. My whole bed was swirling and then there was a serpent lying there. His head was moving and trying to inch towards me the whole time. Chomping at air but something was holding him behind an invisible line that he could not cross. His head was bigger than my hand. I cast him away in Jesus' name and rebuked him and he was gone after a few minutes.

After that, I saw the same repeating vision of the bodies that looked like ants crawling on each other but this time it was like a wall or screen of them, and they were moving sort of as if with a breeze.

Night 2 of visions:

This time a scene of all white – Holy. There was a throne, but I couldn't see faces as it was far off. But I could see other people there in the throne room. Below it looked like those same people crawling on each other, that is my repeating vision. But this time, they were trying to crawl up there into the throne room. Then again, it was like a wall of them swaying like water or in a breeze.

Then I saw a concert. I couldn't tell who it was, I just saw a guy with the guitar walking around in the audience. Then it was chaos. People getting beat up and mass panic with people running everywhere.

Scene then moved to someone in their home being violently beat up by several people.

Morning 3 visions:

I was sitting outside in the sun and I saw the clouds start to come together in a strange manner. The sun got really bright and out of it came a figure all in white with sparkling gold around it holding a book. It was beautiful and I said "Lord, how beautiful you are". And he just stayed suspended there for a while and then went away.

I closed my eyes and the same pink that surrounded me in bed I could see. Movement with rays all around it then rising and rising. It turned into a pink, cloudy tunnel with light at the end of it. Not unlike what the people in my visions are crawling over each other trying to get to.

Then I see the bad guy, the bad eye, the serpent/dragon staring at me. I asked God to make him go away. Then there was a lamb. But he was off to the side, and I couldn't see him real clearly. I believe this to be the dragon pretending to be the lamb as I've warned you guys.

After, I saw the white image with the gold right next to the sun again.

Night 4 of visions:

Many, many evil visions. Most were things that I had seen before and already described here. A new one was a serpent coming down from the ceiling. I believe all of this is preparation and testing so that I won't be (and you won't be) afraid in the future. The whole time, I was just singing, praising, praying and worshiping with whatever the Spirit gave me in that minute. My favorite one that I blurted out towards the end was, "bring it on because you can't do anything to me unless He allows you to!!". And, you know what? That's the truth!

This was the scripture on my journal that day:

Psalm 27:1 The Lord is my light and my salvation – who shall I fear? The Lord is the strong hold of my life – of whom shall I be afraid?

I then saw the bodies again… This time it turned into a big orgy with bodies all over each other. They were then thrown down into the underworld. I didn't see flames, but it was like a hot cave of banishment and I could see bodies being dragged off.

Morning 5 vision: (5 is the number of Grace by the way)

The next morning at sunrise, I saw that same pink that had been comforting me all around the sun and then going up as high as you can see. There was a figure inside that went all the way up into the sky. The sun was just a tiny orb underneath him. Truly majestic and beautiful… there was even shimmering inside the pink. I believe there really is just a thin veil between this world and heaven.

Ephesians 4:10 He that descended is the same also that ascended up far above all heavens, that he might fill all things.

This was obviously the real thing. The other small, white, gold, shiny thing was fake the other day, but even I called him Lord. He was coming out of the sun. Pray constantly and keep your spiritual eyes open.

Another beautiful revelation on this sunrise. If you stare at the sun in the morning, you will see a tunnel of love begin to manifest in pinkish colors. Then, the sun will have a bright light that will begin to encircle it. Not unlike conception or our big bang. Everything with God is pregnant. A new creation every… single… day.

I broke the fast the next day (a total of seven days). The day after that, we went out for pizza as it was my friend's birthday here where I'm staying. That evening as we were driving home after pizza, a ball of fire (a foot around) about 4 feet off the ground went across the road in front of us. She didn't see it, so I didn't say anything. I have no idea what it was or even what to say about it, but God wanted me to put it in here so there you have it.

Well, as usual, He always keeps you guessing. About 2 weeks later, He asked me to fast again. I had been having trouble sleeping. (Imagine that after those visions!) I prayed every night for protection and repented of my fear. But, I was still struggling. So when He asked me to do it again, I wasn't happy about it. But of course, I had to be obedient at this point.

Five days and nothing but sweetness. The same pinkish/redish beautiful eye that follows me inside mine when I shut my eyes with love and peace. Total comfort and security. I interpreted that to mean that He wanted to change my memories of fasting.

So that I wouldn't be afraid to do it again. That is why He did it. And it was a beautiful experience. The details of that are for me. I just realized the five days... and five is the number of grace. He loves us so much.

The next night after I broke it, here come the visions again. Apparently, you don't have to be fasting. Of course, He is God, He can make you see anything, anytime He wants to! I, in no way, pretend to know what any of this means because I even had trouble writing it all down immediately after. But, He instructed me to put it in here so... this is exactly how it reads in my journal:

Many visions tonight. So many I'm not sure what order or even if this was all of them.

-White long thing with like white soft tubes all over it. Looked like something out of the ocean. Then it had friends and one kinda had a face more like a butt really but they surrounded my face.

- Black long snake looking things swaying from ceiling and going past me. Later <u>all</u> over the room and bed.

- White cloudy figures surrounding the bed in a circle.

- More ants/people. This time definitely on a screen then more colors behind this time. Later turned into them swimming around in like a cloud all over the room. Almost looked like espuma, but bodies throughout with heads and arms trying to get out.

- Almost like whitish-silver ticker tape and then started to turn into shapes. The center started twirling. It looked like it was becoming beautiful then it got fat and then lost lustre and just turned into something with its back towards me with a brown coat

- Beautiful white billowy feather looking things over me swaying

The next day He highlighted this scripture for me.

2 Peter 2:17 These are wells without water, clouds that are carried with a tempest; to whom the mist of darkness is reserved for ever.

Also, having had several of these "dark" visions, I started to get a little bold and mouthy. Probably so far as you could even call it tempting the devil. I was convicted this morning by Him that I am NOT to do that. Even the angels don't do that, and I am (and you are) to follow Michael's example in Jude.

Jude 1:9 Yet Michael the archangel, when contending with the devil he disputed about the body of Moses, durst not bring against him a railing accusation, but said, The Lord rebuke thee.

Jannes and Jambres have been put before me by the Holy Spirit many times in the last few months. By tradition, these were the two chief magicians that went up against Moses and Aaron in front of pharaoh. But their names are not mentioned in Exodus, only 2 Timothy. Exodus only says there were many wise men and magicians. What I didn't remember was that for many of the miracles/plagues that God sent, the magicians were able to do them also. This is all summarized from Exodus 7-11:

Aaron's rod became a serpent; Magicians rods became serpents and Aaron's serpent ate theirs.

God through Aaron's rod made the waters blood; And the magicians did so with their enchantments and pharaoh's heart was hardened.

God through Aaron's rod made the frogs come out of the waters; And the magicians did so with their enchantments (Here pharaoh asked Moses and Aaron to ask their God to get rid of them) Then, after God had killed them, and there was respite, pharaoh's heart was hardened.

God through Aaron's rod brought lice from the dust of the land; And the magicians did so with their enchantments and could not. They then told pharaoh this is the finger of God, but his heart was hardened.

God sent the flies upon them; pharaoh agreed to let them go and then hardened his heart after Moses asked God to get rid of the flies and He did.

God sent the plague on the cattle killing the Egyptian's cattle but not Israel's; pharaoh's heart still hardened.

God sent the boils through Moses' sprinkling of ashes toward heaven in pharaoh's site; and the magicians could not stand before Moses because of the boils. This time it says:

Exodus 9:12 And the Lord hardened the heart of pharaoh, and he hearkened not unto them; as the Lord had spoken unto Moses.

The LORD in control this whole time and hardening the heart of pharaoh.

God then sent thunder, hail and fire through Moses hand extended towards heaven; Again, pharaoh asked Moses to ask God to stop it which he did and then hardened his heart.

God told Moses to stretch out his hand to bring the locusts and he stretched out his rod; Again, pharaoh asked Moses to ask God to stop it which he did and then hardened his heart.

God told Moses to stretch out his hand toward heaven to bring the darkness for three days; He considered letting them go and then again, his heart was hardened.

God took the firstborn of everything but spared anyone with the lamb's blood over the door.

All of this to say that the first couple of plagues, the magicians could emulate. You can be assured that satan loves to pretend to be God and will have all of his magic on full display. So, be prepared to see "miracles" from the first christ that comes along. It will be very convincing, but you will know better because you have read the Word and heeded the warnings by Jesus.

I actually believe the whole story of Exodus is an example for our lives today and what is about to happen. You are living under slavery to sin held in place by satan whether you are aware of it or not. I believe you could literally insert satan for pharaoh and that is what you are going to see. (with a rapture thrown in there) Yes, Jannes and Jambres and the other magicians could keep up for the first couple of plagues. But then God, in all His majesty shows them without a doubt who is in charge.

Like pharaoh, God will harden satan's heart. Yes, he controls him too. God has to go through all of this to get the very, very stubborn of his children to turn back to him. They need a show for them to have faith. Remember, He lost not a one. And He won't.

Jesus was in control of satan even during his betrayal before the crucifixion.

John 13:2 And supper being ended, the devil having now put into the heart of Judas Iscariot, Simon's son, to betray him;

John 13:21-27 When Jesus had thus said, he was troubled in spirit, and testified, and said, Verily, verily, I say unto you, that one of you shall betray me. Then the disciples looked one on another, doubting of whom he spake. Now there was leaning on Jesus' bosom one of his disciples, whom Jesus loved. Simon Peter therefore beckoned to him, that he should ask who it should be of whom he spake. He then lying on Jesus' breast saith unto him, Lord, who is it? Jesus answered, He it is, to whom I shall give a sop, when I have dipped it. And when he had dipped the sop, he gave it to Judas Iscariot, the son of Simon. And after the sop Satan entered into him. Then said Jesus unto him, That thou doest, do quickly.

A lot of people think that there will be wars at this time. Actually, Jesus states the opposite.

Matthew 24: 6-8 And ye shall hear of wars and rumours of wars: see that ye be not troubled: for all these things must come to pass, but the end is not yet. For nation shall rise against nation, and kingdom against kingdom: and there shall be famines, and pestilences, and earthquakes, in divers places. All these are the beginning of sorrows.

Sorrows are birth pains (or plagues). The birth pains of God's kingdom coming into being.

Daniel even goes a bit further and says that the devil will come in peacefully and prosperously. By peace he shall destroy many…

Daniel 8:25 And through his policy also he shall cause craft to prosper in his hand; and he shall magnify himself in his heart, and by peace shall destroy many: he shall also stand up against the Prince of princes; but he shall be broken without hand.

These are very serious times, and you do not have the power NOT TO CHOOSE this time. There is no sitting on the sidelines. You either choose life or death. Time is short…

Chapter 17

The Coat of Many Colors

I go through phases in my prayer life. Sometimes I can really feel God working and it encourages me to pray more. Then, I get to praying about everything and I think this is getting kinda crazy. Maybe it's too much. Then, I start thinking its futile because God is God and He is going to do what He wants to do anyway. In His will... So, is it really making a difference?

Then, something will happen, or He will speak through someone in my life about the importance of prayer and I start the cycle over. But I'm never truly understanding what or why I'm doing it.

God knows that we do not know how to pray as we should...

Romans 8:26 Likewise the Spirit also helpeth our infirmities: for we know not what we should pray for as we ought: but the Spirit itself maketh intercession for us with groanings which cannot be uttered

The Holy Spirit literally fills in the blanks for us and makes our prayers acceptable to the Lord. I don't know how that happens, but I have faith that it does. I've been spiritually low several times and actually asked the Holy Spirit to pray for me because I didn't even know what to pray for... that prayer has actually been said many times over this book. And then a sweet peace would come over me and a precious thought to include.

One of those precious thoughts that has been revealing itself over the last several months is the story of Joseph and the Coat of Many Colors. I've heard preachers talk about Joseph as a type or example of Christ. He went before his brothers and sisters and was "killed" by them. He then went into a land to prepare a place for them where he could save them when the famine came. Much like Jesus went and prepared a place for us after He was betrayed. Where He could save our souls by the spiritual food that will be poured out in the end.

I believe we are literally made in God's image. I don't think that verse means that we look like Him. I think we are all a part of Him. I think that Coat of Many Colors reserved for Joseph is a parable for all of God's children that will be stitched together in the priestly robe of Christ.

Romans 8:29 For whom he did foreknow, he also did predestinate to be conformed to the image of his Son, that he might be the firstborn among many brethren.

And, I believe the way that we stitch each other together is by prayer. How precious and mysterious it is. God himself orchestrating each relationship to make that full priestly robe exist together in love and forgiveness. It has taken thousands of years, and he will not miss one stitch.

Colossians 2:2-3 That their hearts might be comforted, being knit together in love, and unto all riches of the full assurance of understanding, to the acknowledgement of the mystery of God, and of the Father, and of Christ; In whom are hid all the treasures of wisdom and knowledge.

I've told you about my recurring vision of the bodies in the dark struggling to reach a light. I think those bodies in the shadows can go both ways. The Choice. We can crawl towards Him or crawl away from Him into eternal darkness.

The words in Hebrew for the "image of God" is Tzelem Elohim. Tzelem is related to the word Tzel which means shadow. Elohim is God. So, we are literally in God's shadow. I think that is beautiful imagery of His constant covering of us.

This choice is also portrayed in "beauty and bands", which I have contemplated for years. You know how sometimes verses or ideas will stick in your mind. This has been that for me. I don't think I still fully understand it yet, but here is the verse.

Zechariah 11:7 And I will feed the flock of slaughter, even you, O poor of the flock. And I took unto me two staves; the one I called Beauty, and the other I called Bands; and I fed the flock.

God created both Beauty (Jesus) and bands (satan). All to teach us... like a good father does. You can lead with love but sometimes you have to use the "bands" to discipline your children. Here is beauty.

Romans 8:35-37 Who shall separate us from the love of Christ? shall tribulation, or distress, or persecution, or famine, or nakedness, or peril, or sword? As it is written, For thy sake we are killed all the day long; we are accounted as sheep for the slaughter. Nay, in all these things we are more than conquerors through him that loved us.

When I was in Greece, I felt a strong pull to go to this one church that was on top of a very large hill. It was not an easy path up there. Many, many stairs only to find at the top of which I realized, I could have taken a cab. But it's all in the journey isn't it dear ones.

It was a very small church with a gorgeous view. Once inside, I realized why the Holy Spirit had guided me there. Here is the beauty and bands.

    This world is quite literally a tug of war for your souls. When your too weak to pull on the beauty to get back closer to God, your Christian brothers and sisters can pray for you. Those prayers will literally draw you closer to Him and out of the clutches of the bands and the ways of this earth and the prince of it.

    Why do you think those were the first two commandments. Love Me first.

John 12:32 And I, if I be lifted up from the earth, will draw all men unto me.

And then, love each other like yourself. In essence, care about each other's salvation as you do your own. And you will stitch them into the family and draw them ALL to Me.

Colossians 3:13-15 Forbearing one another, and forgiving one another, if any man have a quarrel against any: even as Christ forgave you, so also do ye. And above all these things put on charity, which is the bond of perfectness. And let the peace of God rule in your hearts, to the which also ye are called in one body; and be ye thankful.

If you picture as you are praying for someone, that you are actually pulling them out of satan's hands and placing them into Jesus' hands. I guarantee you, your prayer life will take on a whole new meaning.

Here is the end of the bands.

Ezekiel 38:22 And I will plead against him with pestilence and with blood; and I will rain upon him, and upon his bands, and upon the many people that are with him, an overflowing rain, and great hailstones, fire, and brimstone.

Chapter 18

The Woman at the Well

John 4:5-29 Then cometh he to a city of Samaria, which is called Sychar, near to the parcel of ground that Jacob gave to his son Joseph. Now Jacob's well was there. Jesus therefore, being wearied with his journey, sat thus on the well: and it was about the sixth hour. There cometh a woman of Samaria to draw water: Jesus saith unto her, Give me to drink. (For his disciples were gone away unto the city to buy meat.) Then saith the woman of Samaria unto him, How is it that thou, being a Jew, askest drink of me, which am a woman of Samaria? for the Jews have no dealings with the Samaritans. Jesus answered and said unto her, If thou knewest the gift of God, and who it is that saith to thee, Give me to drink; thou wouldest have asked of him, and he would have given thee living water. The woman saith unto him, Sir, thou hast nothing to draw with, and the well is deep: from whence then hast thou that living water? Art thou greater than our father Jacob, which gave us the well, and drank thereof himself, and his children, and his cattle? Jesus answered and said unto her, Whosoever drinketh of this water shall thirst again: But whosoever drinketh of the water that I shall give him shall never thirst; but the water that I shall give him shall be in him a well of water springing up into everlasting life. The woman saith unto him, Sir, give me this water, that I thirst not, neither come hither to draw. Jesus saith unto her, Go, call thy husband, and come hither. The woman answered and said, I have no husband. Jesus said unto her, Thou hast well said, I have no husband: For thou hast had five husbands; and he whom thou now hast is not thy husband: in that saidst thou truly. The woman saith unto him, Sir, I perceive that thou art a prophet. Our fathers worshipped in this mountain; and ye say, that in Jerusalem is the place where men ought to worship. Jesus saith unto her, Woman, believe me, the hour cometh, when ye shall neither in this mountain, nor yet at Jerusalem, worship the Father. Ye worship ye know not what: we know what we worship: for salvation is of the Jews. But the hour cometh, and now is, when the true worshippers shall worship the Father in spirit and in truth: for the Father seeketh such to worship him. God is a Spirit: and they that worship him must worship him in spirit and in truth. The woman saith unto him, I know that Messias cometh, which is called Christ: when he is come, he will tell us all things. Jesus saith unto her, I that speak unto thee am he. And upon this came his disciples, and marvelled that he talked with the woman: yet no man said, What seekest thou? or, Why talkest thou with her? The woman then left her waterpot, and went her way into the city, and saith to the men, Come, see a man, which told me all things that ever I did: is not this the Christ?

I know that was a lot, but I think that story is very important for many, many reasons. One of the main things that stand out to me is, was she ashamed after Jesus sat there and went over everything she had ever done in her life? It says that she dropped the water pot and ran to go tell everyone! Do you think she would have done that if He had shamed her?

No, He told her everything she did and then followed it up with… and here is why you did it. And then, I understand and forgive you! I heal you from all of that hurt and shame and guilt that you have been carrying around all of these years. He set her free.

How do I know all of these things? Because He's done it with me…

I'm going to tell you my most horrible wretched sins. Because He told me to…

Believe me, I prayed about this a lot hoping to get out of it! But some of you probably have the same sins, that you may think are unforgiveable. Or perhaps even worse… have never forgiven yourself. That is possible… and if Jesus forgives you, who are you to hang on to it? Let it go and be free of it! We are supposed to lift each other up. And all sins are forgivable if you ASK forgiveness and turn your life towards Him. So deep breath and here it goes…

I've done a lot of things that I'm not proud of…

Like the woman at the well, I've had many "husbands". I wasn't always that way. I was a virgin until I was about twenty years old. I fell in love with a boy in college and happily lost my virginity. I thought that he was it and we would be married.

Well, that wasn't it and much of it was my fault. I got drunk one night, out with friends and family. One of my brother's friends cornered me in the bathroom. My boyfriend came in through the door and found us kissing. I didn't even like this guy and had only been in there a few minutes from what I can remember. Things were very fuzzy.

He eventually forgave me, but it broke the trust and ruined our relationship. He was older also and graduated before me and that distance eventually killed us. I was devastated.

God knew why it was important to wait until after marriage to have sex. Once you lose your virginity that is it. You can never have that innocence back. Men look at you different and you look at yourself different. That whole lust thing becomes a part of it. Once that hunger is awakened in you it needs to be fed and that goes ten times for men and their libido.

But for a woman, it's not only the urge to have sex… that now is how we are trained to get male affection. And that folks, is messed up. We are designed to need each other. God even said it is not good for man to be alone. That is why he made Adam and Eve because they needed each other.

But now our society (satan), has turned that into being a sign of weakness. You can't be needy in a relationship, or no one will be with you. What?? That makes no sense. Of course I'm needy. I literally have a hole in my body that is supposed to be physically filled with my husband that God picked out for me. Same for him. That is a crazy lie!

We need each other and we need God.

God brought to my mind all of these things in the past few years. He reminded me of my innocence and how and why I started not to respect myself anymore and give myself away. He understood it and it grieved him. And… He reminded me that it grieved me. It was the precious healing that I needed.

He even convicted me to forgive that guy in the bathroom, who is dead at the present time. Even in death they require forgiveness, if they are going to be weaved into that coat of many colors with us. No room for grudges there. How my life would have changed had that not happened. I probably wouldn't be writing this book. Everything happens under His control and for a reason.

As a matter of fact, I think that is really the level of forgiveness that He asks of us. Are you so mad that you want that person cast into hell forever? What kind of person does that make you? Or, do you leave it up to the one who made them and knows their heart. He knows who will be in that robe or not, and you have to have the forgiving heart to make it in there yourself.

That forgiveness that He offers is not to accuse you or hold you responsible. It is to heal you. To heal you completely and totally from the reasons that you did any of those things in the first place. He knows who to hold responsible for all of it.

The worst thing I ever did in my life was to have an abortion in college.

The details of that are unnecessary here, but what is necessary for me to talk about is how deceptive satan is on this topic.

At that point in my life, I thought it would ruin my life. I could never use the education that I was receiving to make anything of myself. I was selfish.

On top of that, I bought into the lies that satan spins around that topic. I thought as the world teaches, that the embryo is not really a baby until much later in the pregnancy. That the first few months it is like a seed and not really anything. Nothing more than having a period really. This is the lie that is believed by much of the world today.

I am embarrassed to say that I didn't really think too much about it at that point because it was early, and I thought of it as not a big deal. Nothing more than a period really and a small seed. That's what I told myself anyway… Just handle it and move on.

But it was always in the back of my mind. Especially as I got older and would see my friend's kids and think how old mine would have been.

I didn't fully grasp what I did until I got back into studying the bible. As soon as Mary became pregnant with Jesus, immediately after conception, she ran to her cousin Elizabeth's house who was pregnant with John the Baptist.

Luke 1:41 And it came to pass, that, when Elisabeth heard the salutation of Mary, the babe leaped in her womb; and Elisabeth was filled with the Holy Ghost:

I refer you back to the moment of conception that we discussed earlier when that light enters the egg. That is the Spirit, and it happens instantly. You are not just stopping a pregnancy, you are stopping a soul from coming into this world. This grieved me to my core.

Especially because later in life I was unable to have children. I thought God was punishing me for what I had done.

One day I was sitting outside feeling sorry for myself because I hadn't conceived. I was married at the time and that was still a possibility. This is the only other time that I "heard" God's voice, and He said to me... "Maybe that is not the plan I have for you". Clear as day. The tone was very much, "so quit feeling sorry for yourself and get to work."

I washed my face and guess I did... About a year later, we were at my mother's eightieth birthday party and she began to lament a little about how sad she was that I had never had children and would have wanted that for me. But she said, you know what, God came to me and told me "Maybe that is not the plan I have for her".

I almost dropped my cake. The exact words...

So, if we break this down... what I had tormented myself about. That abortion many years ago. He knew I was going to have, and He knew how He was going to use it and work it into His plan for me. Amazing Grace.

Then after I had refocused my life again to Him... He brought the father of that soul to my house to apologize for how everything had happened. How he had gotten another girl pregnant at the same time and had told me that he was going to marry her before I had a chance to tell him that I was pregnant. I had completely forgotten that part in the process of beating myself up and not forgiving myself.

But God hadn't forgot, and He knew that piece of information was important for my healing. It was important to help me forgive myself. To communicate to me that He understood why I did it. Amazing Grace indeed.

The second worse thing I've ever done in my life was to have a couple of homosexual experiences. Please don't mistake that for me judging homosexuals at all.

I'm judging myself, because I am not one. Soberly, I would never even think of doing anything like that because I don't have that desire.

For me to have done that, just shows the power of alcohol and the sorcery and seductive powers that can come in those "spirits". As I stated earlier, it can give the devil a foothold in your life to do things that you wouldn't normally do.

These two sins represent 3 days of the almost 20,000 days that I've lived so far. And satan has put them before me in my mind to shame me most of those days.

This is not how God wants us to live. He doesn't want us to live in regret. He says come admit what you've done and come back to me, and I'll forgive it and It's over. I died so that you don't have to think about those things anymore. The devil will not have power over your mind anymore with me in it. You will begin to see yourself through my eyes. Absolutely Beautiful, Amazing Grace!

The third thing I did was lose myself in grief for several years after losing my parents. I'm not going to say that was a "worse" or bad thing because it was beautifully necessary to get me to where I am today in my walk with Christ. But staying there as long as I did, kept me in satan's tools of isolation, alcohol, and sadness for way too long.

As I stated, I lost both of my parents after very long illnesses into which I poured myself into their care. I had already lost my marriage and the ability to have kids. I think after their death, I just completely lost my identity. Not only because I had nothing to associate myself with anymore, but I knew deep down no one would ever love me that much again. At least not in the flesh.

The crash.

I had lost all hope and sense of myself. The people that relied on me, eventually just gave up waiting for me to get better. I wasn't getting better... I couldn't really see a reason for living. All I did was work and drink wine and watch TV. What's the point?

I fleetingly considered suicide... I had no children. I mean really who was going to miss me.

But I'm not that person and I'm not that selfish. I say that not judging anyone. But I couldn't do that to the people I love and I'm lucky enough to have people that love me.

Mostly, I felt the ever-growing presence of God in all of the loss and tribulation. The solitude made me study the bible and the broken heart made me seek Jesus. A love that would never give up on me. You will never know how much you need God until God is all that you have.

Two words that you wouldn't think go together are beautifully tied in Hebrew. Hope and Wait. Hope is Tiqvah, which is the idea of looking forward to something with confident anticipation. It is derived from the verb Qavah, which means to wait for. But Qavah means more than that. Qavah also means to bind yourself to something. Like twisting two or three cords together to make them unbreakable. So, when Jesus said to wait. He wasn't saying grab a chair and open up a magazine. He was saying bind or wrap yourself in me, in that hope which is the promise wherein comes your confidence. Wherein is your HOPE.

I have asked forgiveness of all these things, and I know that He has forgiven me. And He will do that for you if you ask Him.

Isaiah 54:4 Fear not; for thou shalt not be ashamed: neither be thou confounded; for thou shalt not be put to shame: for thou shalt forget the shame of thy youth, and shalt not remember the reproach of thy widowhood any more.

Psalm 25:7 Remember not the sins of my youth, nor my transgressions: according to thy mercy remember thou me for thy goodness' sake, O Lord.

I think the hardest thing in the world is to forgive ourselves. We know right from wrong, and when we mess up the devil is there to ensure that we pay for it, a thousand times over. He amplifies it in our mind. Shouts it, about how awful we are and unlovable, disgusting.

Christ died so we wouldn't have to listen to that crap anymore. I think it goes hand in hand with the reason for prayers. I believe that when we ask for forgiveness, he takes it off of our list and adds it onto the devil's. He knows who to blame for our sins and who convinced us to do them in the first place.

Revelation 8:3-5 And another angel came and stood at the altar, having a golden censer; and there was given unto him much incense, that he should offer it with the prayers of all saints upon the golden altar which was before the throne. And the smoke of the incense, which came with the prayers of the saints, ascended up before God out of the angel's hand. And the angel took the censer, and filled it with fire of the altar, and cast it into the earth: and there were voices, and thunderings, and lightnings, and an earthquake.

Jesus promises that if we confess our sins that our Father is faithful to forgive them.

1 John 7-10 But if we walk in the light, as he is in the light, we have fellowship one with another, and the blood of Jesus Christ his Son cleanseth us from all sin. If we say that we have no sin, we deceive ourselves, and the truth is not in us. If we confess our sins, he is faithful and just to forgive us our sins, and to cleanse us from all unrighteousness. If we say that we have not sinned, we make him a liar, and his word is not in us.

James 5:16 Confess your faults one to another, and pray one for another, that ye may be healed. The effectual fervent prayer of a righteous man availeth much.

This does not mean that you have to go in front of any group at church or otherwise and humiliate yourself. A trusted Christian friend, even one is enough. You will find that once your lungs give breath to it, the power of that sin is gone. Gone forever…

Jesus has already paid for your sins. You may think that your sins are too bad and that you don't deserve forgiveness. I tell you that we all feel that way. After several thousand years at this, I guarantee you that you have not come up with a sin that God hasn't heard of!

He says just to turn away from it in teshuvah, and come back to my open arms and I never want to hear about it again.

Does that mean that I live a perfect life now? Or that you need to, in order to be blessed?

None of us meet that standard and that would mean that we thought we could get into heaven by our own good deeds. It doesn't work that way. Only THE WAY… faith in Jesus. He died because he knew none of us could meet the standard of holiness required to live in his presence. He had to die and His blood, as the ultimate sacrifice, had to cleanse us for us to live in Heaven with Him.

The bible says that He offers us tender mercies every day! He knows we are going to mess up somehow every single day!

But as long as we keep trying to turn ourselves to him completely every day, He forgives us and is with us.

Lamentations 3:22-23 It is of the Lord's mercies that we are not consumed, because his compassions fail not. They are new every morning: great is thy faithfulness.

Amazing Grace. How sweet the sound.

He is in you, He is all around you. He is the very air you breathe… the life giving Ruach spirit that He breathed into your lungs to give you life. He is the gravity that attaches all of us to Him. We are all one in Him.

Thank you for replacing your Ruach to the devil's own condemning breath in mine to myself. And, thank you for your promise to do the same for these reading this Father, that I lay on the altar in front of you.

Chapter 19

Kosmos

Kosmos is a beautiful Greek word that means the universe. (You've probably heard of the Cosmos in English) The verb of that, is Kosmeo in the Greek, which has some beautiful meanings. It means to be adorned, garnished, decorated as in the perfect arrangement and ornament of the heavens and this earth. It is the perfection of His creation.

Since we live in a fallen world, our world is not in perfect order. I'm sure that is stating the obvious to you. As talked about earlier, it is the upside-down of perfect in its current state. Not only fallen, but the opposite of what it should be.

As always, Satan tries to imitate God. So, he "adorns" things too. To dress them up and make them look holy when they are not.

Luke 21:5-6 And as some spake of the temple, how it was adorned with goodly stones and gifts, he said, As for these things which ye behold, the days will come, in the which there shall not be left one stone upon another, that shall not be thrown down.

They even adorn/garnish the tombs of the prophets that they themselves killed!

Matthew 23:29 Woe unto you, scribes and Pharisees, hypocrites! because ye build the tombs of the prophets, and garnish the sepulchres of the righteous,

That beautiful word Kosmeo can also mean to put back in order, in perfect order. This will happen when Christ comes back. He will place everything back into the harmonious order that He created it. All of His creation, the universe and all in it made perfect again. His Kosmos.

Revelation 21:1-4 And I saw a new heaven and a new earth: for the first heaven and the first earth were passed away; and there was no more sea. And I John saw the holy city, new Jerusalem, coming down from God out of heaven, prepared as a bride adorned for her husband. And I heard a great voice out of heaven saying, Behold, the tabernacle of God is with men, and he will dwell with them, and they shall be his people, and God himself shall be with them, and be their God. And God shall wipe away all tears from their eyes; and there shall be no more death, neither sorrow, nor crying, neither shall there be any more pain: for the former things are passed away.

This world will be adorned, made perfect, for its Husband. It says that all creation groans for His return, not only people.

I was watching some program and they had a woman on there that had died. She talked about how everything worships God there in Heaven. The trees, the grass, people, animals… all swaying together in the same worship of the Spirit. Can you imagine?

Not much later, I went on a dive in Florida. While I was underwater, everything was swaying together in the current. The plants, the fish, even me... It made me think, this is like heaven.

How beautiful. Every living thing singing the same song to our Creator.

There is research ongoing that states that our DNA sings. Each DNA nucleotide has a specific frequency spectrum. If those are translated into frequencies that a human ear can hear, it begins to sound like notes, and you can hear music. I don't think this is an accident at all. It is how our spirit will continue to worship in Heaven.

Now that we have gone over adorning the fake way and adorning this world back into perfection, let's talk about how the bride is adorned at the end. How you and me will be made perfect and whole to be presented to Him.

Matthew 25:1-13 Then shall the kingdom of heaven be likened unto ten virgins, which took their lamps, and went forth to meet the bridegroom. And five of them were wise, and five were foolish. They that were foolish took their lamps, and took no oil with them: But the wise took oil in their vessels with their lamps. While the bridegroom tarried, they all slumbered and slept. And at midnight there was a cry made, Behold, the bridegroom cometh; go ye out to meet him. Then all those virgins arose, and trimmed their lamps. And the foolish said unto the wise, Give us of your oil; for our lamps are gone out. But the wise answered, saying, Not so; lest there be not enough for us and you: but go ye rather to them that sell, and buy for yourselves. And while they went to buy, the bridegroom came; and they that were ready went in with him to the marriage: and the door was shut.

As we have already discussed, Jesus is the olive tree and the Anointed One and He is the Word of God. That oil in their lamps is the Word of God and Jesus himself. If He is not in you, you are out. Those others were told to go and buy some oil and of course will never find the kind of oil required to join that wedding for sale. I'm sure they went to false preachers for that oil and there is none there because you can't buy it. You can only accept it into your soul.

That oil has already been paid for by Jesus on the cross.

Those five had adorned themselves for the wedding. They had plenty of oil which means they knew the word of God and had Jesus in them. But, what else did they do?

They trimmed their wicks so their light would be brighter. They got rid of the black stuff at the top. The dross, the sin that was stuck to them from this world dimming their light before they went out and met their Husband. They repented.

Jesus washed the feet of the disciples right before He was betrayed. He symbolically was washing the sin off of them from walking on this Earth but also offering forgiveness and preparing them to stand in Heaven. So, their feet could touch holy ground. AND, telling us to do the same for each other, to forgive and prepare each other for The Way.

John 13:12-15 So after he had washed their feet, and had taken his garments, and was set down again, he said unto them, Know ye what I have done to you? Ye call me Master and Lord: and ye say well; for so I am. If I then, your Lord and Master, have washed your feet; ye also ought to wash one another's feet. For I have given you an example, that ye should do as I have done to you.

These are the things that you need to attend the wedding. Jesus, study and repentance.

Revelation 19:7-9 Let us be glad and rejoice, and give honour to him: for the marriage of the Lamb is come, and his wife hath made herself ready. And to her was granted that she should be arrayed in fine linen, clean and white: for the fine linen is the righteousness of saints. And he saith unto me, Write, Blessed are they which are called unto the marriage supper of the Lamb. And he saith unto me, These are the true sayings of God.

Well, it has taken me this whole book to realize what those ants/people in the shadows are.

Proverbs 6:6-11 Go to the ant, thou sluggard; consider her ways, and be wise: Which having no guide, overseer, or ruler, Provideth her meat in the summer, and gathereth her food in the harvest. How long wilt thou sleep, O sluggard? when wilt thou arise out of thy sleep? Yet a little sleep, a little slumber, a little folding of the hands to sleep: So shall thy poverty come as one that travelleth, and thy want as an armed man.

God is telling us to wake up and get to work. How long will you sleep, how long will you stay in darkness? Gather your food for the winter coming. Stock up your oil of the Word of God and the love and joy of Jesus. Then you will not wake up empty when He comes. You will be stitched into the Coat of many Colors and secure in those fibers of Beauty. You will just sway secured with your brothers and sisters in that storm.

Or, you can find yourself clawing over others to try and make it into that white thrown room only to have the door shut and then be cast down in the underbelly of this world. This is real. I've seen it.

I hope I've convinced you that I'm not (completely) crazy and that God is pleading with you to take action. It is easy action too. Love and read about Me.

Time is short. Repent of your sins today. You've carried that shame long enough and you need to drop that pack and let Jesus pick it up for you. His yoke is light. Pick up your bible and start reading.

I recommend starting with Matthew and then going back to the prophets that prophesied of Christ coming, maybe Isaiah. Keep going back and forth like that. That will increase your faith. That is how I like to do it anyway, but there is no wrong way. Always pray for wisdom and understanding and He will give it to you. I'm living proof of that.

Most of all teshuvah. Turn your whole heart and life to Him. Tell Him you love Him and Thank Him for all of your blessings.

Don't ever forget the will of God for you. It's really not very hard.

1 Thessalonians 5:16-18 Rejoice evermore. Pray without ceasing. In every thing give thanks: for this is the will of God in Christ Jesus concerning you.

You ALL are in my prayers.

John 14:1-4 Let not your heart be troubled: ye believe in God, believe also in me. In my Father's house are many mansions: if it were not so, I would have told you. I go to prepare a place for you. And if I go and prepare a place for you, I will come again, and receive you unto myself; that where I am, there ye may be also. And whither I go ye know, and the way ye know.

John 14:13-21 And whatsoever ye shall ask in my name, that will I do, that the Father may be glorified in the Son. If ye shall ask any thing in my name, I will do it. If ye love me, keep my commandments. And I will pray the Father, and he shall give you another Comforter, that he may abide with you for ever; Even the Spirit of truth; whom the world cannot receive, because it seeth him not, neither knoweth him: but ye know him; for he dwelleth with you, and shall be in you. I will not leave you comfortless: I will come to you. Yet a little while, and the world seeth me no more; but ye see me: because I live, ye shall live also. At that day ye shall know that I am in my Father, and ye in me, and I in you. He that hath my commandments, and keepeth them, he it is that loveth me: and he that loveth me shall be loved of my Father, and I will love him, and will manifest myself to him.

John 14:27-29 Peace I leave with you, my peace I give unto you: not as the world giveth, give I unto you. Let not your heart be troubled, neither let it be afraid. Ye have heard how I said unto you, I go away, and come again unto you. If ye loved me, ye would rejoice, because I said, I go unto the Father: for my Father is greater than I. And now I have told you before it come to pass, that, when it is come to pass, ye might believe.

www.ingramcontent.com/pod-product-compliance
Lightning Source LLC
Chambersburg PA
CBHW061112070526
44583CB00027B/3267